W9-CME-244

THE UNFORGIVEN

The Untold Story of One Woman's Search for Love and Justice

Edith Brady-Lunny
Steve Vogel
Author of best-seller
Reasonable Doubt

To my parents, Barbara and Francis Brady Sr.,
whose story and love live on.
–EB-L

To my wife Mary, our children Rob, Eric and Krista, and
our son-in-law Alex for their love and support.
–SV

Additional information about this case, including actual video and audio introduced in the trials, is available on the authors' websites: www.stevevogelauthor.com and www.edithbradylunny.com.

Also by Steve Vogel:

Reasonable Doubt: A shocking story of lust and murder in the American heartland

Preface

Our society demands we place responsibility where it belongs, insisting on accountability and consequences for errant acts. Yet our culture also embraces forgiveness, as thorny and complicated as it may be.

This is a true story of guilt, of grief, and pain for lives lost, of a reckoning for mistakes that can never be reversed. It's the story about a woman whose life, littered with years of abuse and her own misguided attempts to capture love she desperately craved, took an ugly turn on a single evening and then a despairing path through the halls of justice.

The story spirals full circle in an unforeseen, even bewildering way, confronting you with gnawing questions about fairness and quality of justice, about victims unable to speak for themselves, about the well-being of the most vulnerable, about whether society has been well or poorly served.

Co-author Edith Brady-Lunny is a reporter who witnessed much, if not most, of what's described here. Actual trial transcripts and police recordings are used, edited only for brevity and clarity.

"I can forgive, but I cannot forget"
is only another way of saying,
"I cannot forgive."

Henry Ward Beecher

Chapter One

"Save my babies! Oh my God!"

Amanda Hamm was hysterical, jumping up and down, pointing to the water, screaming her aching plea to the first emergency worker to arrive after her frantic 911 call.

The tall woman with wavy chestnut hair was being held in check by her boyfriend, Maurice LaGrone Jr., his arms wrapped around Amanda's waist. Now he turned her around, forcing her head into his shoulder, trying to prevent her from seeing the desperate scene about to unfold some 70 yards from where they stood.

DeWitt County Sheriff's Department Sergeant Timothy Collins looked toward the waters of Clinton Lake. A vehicle was submerged, not far from a boat ramp. Tail lights—not what he would expect—reflected through the water. Usually it was headlights you'd see when a car or truck, on a slippery ramp, was dragged backwards into the water by an attached boat trailer. This green 1997 Oldsmobile Cutlass had gone into the lake front-end first—not backwards. The hood of the four-door car dipped downward in seven feet of water. The vehicle's rear portion was closer to the shore, resting in water just over four feet deep.

As other rescuers began to arrive, Collins quickly turned to what brought him and the others to the lake at breakneck speeds—saving children trapped inside the submerged car.

He removed his gun belt and ran into the water, noticing part of the car's antenna was above the water. The lake was calm but so murky that when he dove under water, he could see nothing. Collins felt his way along to a door handle on the vehicle's passenger side. He opened the front door with little effort. But the weight of his wet uniform and bullet-proof vest pulled him down. He swam, then waded back to shore where he removed the vest.

Meanwhile a second deputy replaced Collins at the front passenger door. Reaching through the inky water, his hands felt an infant car seat. It was empty. He grabbed it and pushed it behind him. His next desperate reach produced a little girl, not much more than an infant, floating face down in the front portion of the car. He flipped the toddler onto her back and pushed her over to Collins who rushed her to paramedics waiting on the boat ramp.

So began the hand-to-hand relay between first responders who used every ounce of instinct and training to save the children.

A Clinton ambulance pulled into the parking lot with two emergency medical technicians on board. One of them waded into the water and took a second child, a young boy, maybe 50 pounds, from a deputy and hurried him to a partner.

The second EMT performed mouth-to-mouth resuscitation on the boy as she helped carry him from the lake. Once inside the ambulance, the unconscious child vomited frequently, making it difficult to force air into his lungs through an oxygen mask placed on his face. The rescuer did chest compressions, paused to check for a pulse that wasn't returning and screamed for help when the little girl was delivered to the back of the ambulance. Two firefighters responded and immediately applied to the girl the same life-saving maneuvers being used on her brother.

Back in the lake, an EMT was pulling still another boy, younger, from his floating posture in the rear of the car. The boy's feet had been snagged in the tentacles of a seat belt. The emergency responder rushed him to shore, lay him on the ground and began CPR outside the ambulance hectic with activity aimed at saving the boy's brother and sister.

Watching the drama unfold from a fishing boat was Darren Leggett. The timing of his trip back to shore after an evening on the lake had put him in the midst of the turmoil. A woman's screams of "my kids are dead" had competed with the grumble of his boat's motor. Setting aside initial hesitancy to become involved with what looked like a domestic situation between a bi-racial couple, Leggett had moved his boat closer to see what he could do. That's when the first police unit arrived.

Leggett relayed to officers the meager but crucial information he had gleaned from the couple: There were three kids in the car. Now it was obvious to him that the two boys and little girl were all in extreme distress.

As the sun set on the surreal scene, Maurice consoled Amanda, continuing to hold her back from the ambulance and the commotion as the first, second, then third child was pulled from Clinton Lake. They remained near the pay phone they had used to summon help in the parking lot within clear view of the lake.

A Clinton firefighter was behind the wheel of the ambulance as it pulled out for the sprint to Clinton's hospital with six-year-old Christopher, 23-month-old Kyleigh and four rescuers on board. The desperate labor to save the youngsters would continue for all of the five-minute ride.

With a second ambulance not yet at the scene, rescue workers decided to transport three-year-old Austin in the rear of the fire department vehicle. One EMT continued life-saving efforts in the back of the SUV as another firefighter hurried them to the hospital.

It had taken first responders less than two minutes after they arrived to get the kids out of the submerged car. But it was hard to tell how long the children had been in the water. Their small bodies appeared lifeless.

Deputy Bruce Randolph directed Amanda and Maurice into the back seat of his patrol car for the high-speed ride to the hospital.

"Is there somebody we can call?" he asked as the police vehicle tore down Route 10, lights and siren going.

"I can't breathe," Amanda gasped. She was wet and cold. "Do you think my kids will be okay?"

Maurice held her. "Sweet Jesus," he said. "Let these kids be all right."

Randolph was determined to get Amanda to the hospital as quickly as possible in case there were questions she needed to answer for the medical staff. But his haste seemed to add to Maurice's anxiety. Several times he asked the officer to slow down from his speed of 100 mph.

Chapter Two

Dr. David Gill was in the middle of his routine emergency room shift at Clinton's Dr. John Warner Hospital when he heard a police radio dispatch about a multi-victim accident. Additional doctors and nurses were immediately summoned to beef up the small hospital's skeletal medical staff supervised by a single physician.

As the three children arrived in the two emergency vehicles, he recognized them. Their mother brought one or more of them to the ER almost monthly for treatment of what generally was nothing more than a case of the sniffles. Now they were rushed to separate treatment rooms and individually paired with a doctor and nurse prepared to put every shred of their medical knowledge, skill and energy into trying to revive the three children.

The two-story hospital's parking lot was overflowing with emergency vehicles when Randolph's squad car screeched to a stop. He moved quickly through the ER's automatic doors and, looking behind, saw Amanda and Maurice were slow to emerge from the vehicle. Once inside, Amanda rushed to get to her children, but she was stayed by nurses otherwise busy organizing life-saving resources.

Maurice remained closer to the entrance, away from the first-floor hallway and two treatment rooms where the three children were taken. It was already crowded with rescuers, police and even some family members. Amanda's mother Ann Danison and aunt

Kathy Clifton had been brought to the hospital by Ann's fiancé, Lindy Powers. He had been watching TV when he got an urgent call: Bring Amanda's mother to the hospital right away, the receptionist told him, offering no details.

Lindy and Ann were engaged and living in her childhood home on Clinton's north side. With no specifics to offer about the nature of the emergency, Powers pulled Ann and her sister from a church meeting they were attending. Their ailing mother had probably taken a turn for the worse, they speculated, as they drove the few blocks to the hospital. But that thought evaporated as Lindy maneuvered his car through the maze of emergency vehicles. Something was massively wrong, he thought, and it almost certainly didn't involve his fiancé's mother. What they saw was a chaotic nightmare.

When Ann first heard, then spotted her daughter in the hallway, Amanda was screaming and crying, angry because she wasn't being allowed to see her children. As she hugged Amanda, Ann was curious why her daughter's clothing and hair were wet. She saw Maurice further down the hallway, yowling as if he were drunk, a sound unlike any cries Ann had ever heard before.

Overwhelmed with fear and dizziness, Ann couldn't bring herself to ask Amanda what had happened to her grandchildren and was instead helped to a nearby waiting room where she was given oxygen. Amanda passed the hallway but joined her mother periodically, laying her head on her mother's lap and crying, "I want my babies."

Lindy Powers stood by helplessly as he watched utter despair saturate his future wife and stepdaughter. He felt it, too.

Dr. Brit Williams, a physician summoned for the emergency and assigned to Christopher, was guardedly optimistic when rescue workers told him his patient had been in the water about 15 minutes—not so long, he thought, that the boy couldn't be revived.

As he worked on the six-year-old, Dr. Williams determined a blood oxygen level of 20—far below a normal 80 to 100. Warmed liquid packs were applied to the boy's body. Warm saline was infused through an IV in an effort to raise his body temperature above its 92 degrees. The doctor noted Christopher's airway was full of water, a factor that added to his growing skepticism about how long the boy was said to have been underwater.

Meanwhile Dr. Gill was working on Austin, who had arrived with no detectable pulse or blood pressure. Still, the doctor believed the child might be saved.

Blankets were placed over Austin to raise his low body temperature while Dr. Gill tried to restart the boy's heart. Forty-five minutes into the resuscitation effort, the temperature had risen to 98 but the heart would not beat.

Dr. Gill found the boy's mother in the hospital's chapel at the end of the hall and broke the news to her. Austin was gone.

"Oh my God, no! No!" Amanda screamed. She fell to the floor.

With miracles and medical wonders exhausted, doctors pronounced both boys dead at 9:15 p.m.

Dr. Tricia Scerba had been about to sit down to dinner with guests at her Clinton home when Dr. Gill called, asking her to come to the hospital right away to help with the emergency. She had arrived at 8 p.m., minutes before the ambulance, and met with Drs. Gill and Williams. They quickly decided that she, a pediatrician, would care for the youngest victim.

Dr. Scerba, too, began to question the report that the children had been submerged for 15 minutes when she discovered how much water was in the baby's lungs and stomach and its body temperature was only 85 degrees. After 40 minutes of effort, Kyleigh's body temperature had risen to 97 degrees and her heart began to beat sporadically. Dr. Scerba met Amanda in the small chapel. Surrounded by family members, she briefed Amanda on her daughter's grave condition and plans to airlift her to a children's hospital an hour away in Peoria. If Amanda was going to have time with Kyleigh, it needed to happen right away, the doctor told her.

Amanda followed the doctor to the treatment room where the little girl lay on a gurney. "I'm sorry," Amanda said. "I'm sorry," she repeated several times.

Dr. Scerba, seeking a better understanding of what had happened, asked Amanda.

"We went to the lake before going home to watch movies," Amanda told the doctor. "We were getting ready to leave and he got confused on which way. He put it in the wrong gear and hit the gas and we sped into the lake. He got mixed up."

"Did you try to get them out?" the doctor asked.

"It was all tangled." Amanda struggled to put words together. "I couldn't find anything. I'm so sorry."

It was the first of many apologies Amanda would be offering authorities and those closest to the children. They all sought—nearly demanded—an explanation that made more sense, one that more closely mirrored feelings that the mother could have—should have—saved her children.

At 9:40 p.m., a helicopter set down in the parking lot of a nearby Dairy Queen restaurant that served as a landing site for medical transports. A nurse accompanied Kyleigh on the 30-minute flight to St. Francis Medical Center in Peoria.

Trauma produces myriad reactions. Some people are calm and focused, putting all their energy into dealing with what's in front of them. Others become hysterical, draining away any ability to manage the ordeal, replacing it with paralyzing fear and anxiety. With two brothers dead on tables in the emergency room and their little sister clinging to life on a medical transport, questions began to surface in hushed tones and subtle observations among those who responded to the call for help.

"There's something wrong with this," one EMT told Dr. Gill. "We got in there and the water was so shallow. It wasn't hard to get them out."

Detective Rick Hawn, a 10-year-year veteran with the DeWitt County Sheriff's Department, had just finished photographing the nude bodies of Christopher and Austin when Amanda was allowed to see her sons, starting with Austin. Standing in the corner of the treatment room littered with medical supplies spent in the futile attempt to save a life, Hawn closely observed Amanda's demeanor and reactions and those of her cousin, Jackie Blackburn, who was with her.

Blackburn loved her three young relatives but barely tolerated their mother. She considered Amanda an inadequate parent based on multiple relationships that never worked out—most especially her most recent lover. Blackburn couldn't overlook the fact that Maurice's roving eyes had once settled on her.

"I love you Austin," Amanda said to her younger son as she plunged her face into the pillow still supporting his head on the gurney. "I want you to come home with me. Why did this have to happen to you?"

Minutes later in another room, Amanda and her cousin spent time with Christopher. Again, Amanda buried her face in a pillow and didn't look directly at the deceased child.

"I love you so much," she said. Tears did not come. "You were doing so good in school. I never wanted anything to happen to you. I'm so sorry. I tried so hard."

Hawn didn't take his eyes off Amanda. He assessed her every move and how she expressed her grief. His observations, and those of others who witnessed the adrenaline-filled moments at the lake and hospital, would shape perceptions, a lengthy investigation and its conclusions.

Yet those closest to Amanda knew tears and raw emotion had long been extinguished in her as she dealt with the trauma and abuse of her childhood. As an adult, Amanda hid her wounds as best she could, sometimes becoming defensive, almost armored, when life's challenges were more than she could manage.

Hawn, however, was unaware of Amanda's past struggles. He knew only what his instincts as a police officer told him: This situation had the distinct whiff of a potential crime.

The few, final minutes Amanda spent with her sons in the sterile setting of a hospital emergency room came near the end of what had begun as a routine day in a busy household.

As was her habit, Amanda dropped off her three children at 8 a.m. at the parking lot of a grocery store where their babysitter was ending her shift as a crossing guard near Clinton Junior High. The babysitter gave the boys the Pop Tarts their mom had brought with them for breakfast as she took them to Douglas Elementary School. Then she drove to her home where she would look after Kyleigh for the next six hours.

Amanda went to her job at Grecian Gardens Restaurant while Maurice hung out at the apartment, playing video games. The dayslong discord over her suspicions that he was involved with other women had been shrouding their relationship in near silence.

Yet the fear of losing her boyfriend, even one who cheated, kept her in the doomed relationship. Following fights over Maurice's serial infidelity, it was always Amanda who went back.

After her restaurant shift ended at 2 p.m., Amanda stopped by a fast food restaurant a few blocks away to check on the status of her application for a second job. With no word available on the job, she went on to pick up Kyleigh from the sitter's and go home until it was time to fetch the boys at school. She changed clothes, trying to avoid Maurice's obvious frustration as she ignored him. She lacked the energy to initiate an argument over what was bothering her.

Amanda left the apartment with Kyleigh to get the boys and run a few payday errands.

She visited the housing authority office to make a payment on her overdue rent balance of 313 dollars. Tight finances continually put Amanda behind on her government-subsidized monthly rent of 142 dollars.

At a bank drive-up window, Amanda cashed two child support checks and made a payment on her six-year-old Cutlass before going to the DeWitt County courthouse where her mother worked as a secretary in the state's attorney's office. Amanda wanted to repay the 15 dollars she had borrowed from her mom earlier that week.

Christopher tapped on the window outside Ann's office to get his grandma's attention. He waved the money in his hand. Ann stepped outside to see her daughter and the other children who waited in the car. As always, the kids were thrilled to see her. Austin asked if he could spend the night with her, a request she turned down because she and Lindy were still unpacking boxes from their recent move into her childhood home.

"It's my turn anyway," Christopher reminded his brother.

It would be the last time Ann Danison would see her grandchildren alive.

In her final stop before going home, Amanda went by her Aunt Kathy's house to talk to Kathy's boyfriend about moving a bed to Amanda's home for Kyleigh.

Back at the apartment, Maurice pressed Amanda for the reason for her chilly mood. She believed he knew. She also believed no good could come from talking about it just then.

Family dinner plans centered on the orange chicken Amanda planned to make. But her frustration grew when she was unable to find the cookbook with the recipe. Macaroni and cheese was a possibility, but Amanda suggested they take the children out to eat. It was, after all, payday, Sept. 2, 2003. And the day before the anniversary of their first date.

Tension followed the family into The Shack, a diner and Clinton's oldest restaurant. As they occupied a booth near the door, eyes turned toward Maurice, as usual the only minority in the restaurant. He knew there would be stares. In Clinton, it was one thing to have a black man in the restaurant. It was something more for that black man to be with a white woman.

Before she sat down, Amanda went to use the restroom. Christopher and Austin followed. Kyleigh stayed behind, her high chair next to Maurice.

The waitress took drink orders from Maurice for the entire group: a lemonade for him, a Coke for Amanda, milk for the children. The waitress sensed disharmony between the two adults as Amanda and the boys returned from the restroom and the family awaited dinner.

Eager to finish his food and leave an uncomfortable environment made worse by the domestic discord, Maurice ignored the chit chat among the children about their food.

There was even disagreement about what to do after dinner. Maurice was interested in picking up some movies, getting the kids to bed and relaxing. It was still early, Amanda argued, her dream of the life she wanted for her family—happy times shared with children—again colliding with her boyfriend's desires. She suggested they take the kids to Clinton Lake before calling it a night on a nice fall evening.

Maurice grudgingly agreed, pushing the speed limit as he drove east on Route 10. It was the first time he and Amanda had gone to the lake together. Amanda gave him directions, telling him to turn off the highway onto an asphalt-paved road lined with autumn-toned trees.

The west side access to the lake has an upper level parking lot where boaters park their vehicles and trailers. Maurice drove past the lot, down a hill towards the lake, stopping the car on the boat ramp, facing the water. The car's front bumper was close to the water's edge, offering the car's occupants a perfect view of the lake.

What happened next traumatized and divided the community. It also put Amanda and Maurice on a collision course with the criminal justice system and a fight for their lives.

Chapter Three

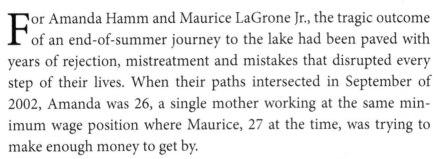

For Amanda Hamm and Maurice LaGrone Jr., the tragic outcome of an end-of-summer journey to the lake had been paved with years of rejection, mistreatment and mistakes that disrupted every step of their lives. When their paths intersected in September of 2002, Amanda was 26, a single mother working at the same minimum wage position where Maurice, 27 at the time, was trying to make enough money to get by.

The search for a stable life started early for Amanda. Growing up in the central Illinois town of 7,000 that gave its name to the nearby lake, Amanda was 11 years old when her mother, Ann, married Mark Walston, a utility company worker who cared enough to adopt Amanda. Her natural father had left the family when she was three. He surrendered parental rights after her mother married Walston.

The emotional pain brought on by her biological father's abandonment stayed with Amanda and worsened when her mother and adoptive father split after eight years.

Lingering trauma and upheaval in her family life led Amanda to her first suicide attempt at age 14; she was hospitalized after swallowing 42 aspirin.

Learning difficulties put her on a special education track in school and left her feeling apart from other students, especially popular girls able to choose their friends and turn down dates Amanda was never offered. Thin and nearly six feet tall, she was taunted by classmates who called her "Stork."

Amanda was chronically late for school because she stopped to smoke behind a convenience store. She faked being ill to avoid classes and received a letter just two months before graduation threatening expulsion. So, she dropped out and later obtained a high school equivalency certificate. With her functioning ability ranked on the low average end of the IQ scale by school counselors, the certificate spoke more to Amanda's determination to support herself financially than her skills as a student.

Having watched her mother rotate among romantic relationships, Amanda craved the attention and affection of men. She sought proof she was worthy of love. Her abuse as a child and later as a young woman surely colored her relationships with male partners. Always the goal was to find a man whose love would be loyal and long lasting. If she could find that devotion, Amanda would cling to it as bedrock for the stable family she yearned for but was denied as a child. Her reckless and often desperate search for a partner produced the opposite results: three pregnancies in six years with three different men.

From their conception, Christopher, Austin and Kyleigh sailed along rocky shores. Amanda had met Christopher's father, Greg Hamm, while they both worked temp jobs obtained thorough an employment agency and married in February of 1997. Little Christopher was born three months later. Within two years, they were divorced. A half-year relationship with Craig Brown produced Austin in November 1999. An even shorter interlude with Shane Senters, a man she had known for about a decade, resulted in the birth of Kyleigh less than two years after that.

Each time, sex preceded commitment, and when the sex ended, so did the relationship. Amanda found herself alone after each disappointment, working two, sometimes three, minimum wage jobs to pay the bills. The series of missteps had proved costly for her—economically and emotionally.

Maurice LaGrone Jr. was equally trapped by his dysfunctional background.

As he entered his teen years in St. Louis, Maurice watched a drug habit swallow up his mother. Doris Woodley disappeared for weeks at a time. She sought treatment yet slipped deeper into the dark world of crack cocaine. Maurice was sent to live within a circle of family members, developing a strong connection with younger cousins.

At 15, he was shuffled north to Bloomington, Ill., to stay with his father and stepmother. Maurice loved music, especially singing. Church activities at the Living Word Church occupied much of his time. There was choir practice on Tuesdays and Saturdays, Bible study classes on Wednesdays and services on Sunday. School work was not a priority.

The addictions to alcohol and crack cocaine that controlled the life of Maurice's mother had the same stranglehold on his father. He watched as his dad, sitting in a living room chair, sorted marijuana seeds. Maurice described the move from the family chaos in St. Louis to Bloomington as "a jump out of the jelly into a jam."

Maurice had a knack when it came to convincing women that he was there for them—at least for the amount of time he was willing to invest in the relationship.

Such an opportunity with a 17-year-old girl swayed Maurice to drop out of Bloomington High School during his junior year. He was just 16 when he took up with the young woman, whose status as a single mother was the start of a pattern for Maurice. At three years, it was to be his longest-lasting relationship, one in which she trusted Maurice to babysit her infant son, who came to call him "dad." He also held a string of minimum wage jobs.

At age 20, Maurice was grief stricken but not surprised when he received word his mother's body had been found in a dumpster in St. Louis. Police believed she had been beaten to death with a shovel. A suspect was later convicted of her rape and murder.

When Maurice's relationship with the young woman ended, he returned to St. Louis where he lived with an aunt until he met and began a relationship with another young woman. The couple had a son who bore Maurice's name. At two months of age and sleeping between his parents, the baby died of what was determined to be Sudden Infant Death Syndrome. Not long after that, the couple broke up over the same issues that eventually toppled all of Maurice's matches with women—an immaturity that led to an inability to keep a steady job.

Within a few months, Maurice had met and moved in with another single mother and her two children in a Farmington, Mo., apartment. He stayed two years before she grew tired of paying all the bills.

With other doors closed, Maurice returned to his father's home in June 2002 where he shared cramped quarters with several stepbrothers and cousins. He was now 27.

Had Maurice compiled a work resume, it would have reflected a series of short-term jobs at fast food restaurants and temp positions where his pay averaged $6 an hour. It was at one of those jobs—a bulk mail packaging company in Heyworth, a small-town midway between Bloomington and Clinton—that he met Amanda Hamm.

At first, Maurice hardly noticed his co-worker, even though they worked side-by-side assembling packets of printed material for an insurance company. But after a while, her obvious attraction to him was hard to ignore. After all, he hadn't had sex in weeks. They slept together on their first date on Sept. 3, 2002.

Amanda and her three children were living in a three-bedroom public housing apartment on Clinton's east edge. Each morning she would drive 30 miles north to Bloomington to pick up her new boyfriend and then double-back 12 miles south to their jobs in Heyworth. After about a week, they agreed he should move in. For Maurice, it represented a liberated lifestyle, away from his father and stepmother.

There were several other low-wage jobs that came and went before Amanda and Maurice both got work at the Grecian Gardens Restaurant near their apartment, she waiting tables for $3.09 an hour plus tips, he washing dishes for $5.15 an hour.

From its start, the courtship of Maurice and Amanda was risky business. Not long after Maurice moved into her apartment, Amanda's friends and relatives became wary of her new relationship. Yes, Maurice seemed to enjoy playing with the children, but his refusal to watch them while Amanda worked or ran errands put him in disfavor with Amanda's mother. Besides, there was an impulsive side that made him less than a reliable caretaker for the children. Christopher and Austin told their babysitter about games Maurice played that involved knives and pretending to put their heads in the oven. Beyond that, Ann worried her daughter's decision to date a black man could be an issue for her grandchildren in a town where African-Americans were less than one percent of the population.

Finances were tight. Food stamps worth 300 dollars supplemented the two restaurant paychecks and a total of about 400 dollars in monthly child support from the children's three fathers—all stretched thin to pay the costs of housing and medical care not covered by public assistance. Yet cash was found for alcohol and drugs. Maurice liked a steady stream of marijuana, a drug Amanda also enjoyed as a way to relax.

Arguments flared over Maurice's demands for frequent sex, over previous relationships and what might be going on when Amanda was at work. Friends believed the disputes sometimes turned physical. On at least three occasions, they saw Amanda with a blackened eye or bruises on her neck.

But the two stayed together for the limited benefits the other brought to the relationship. Amanda would never give up her dream of a functional family and even firmed up plans to attend a private college in downtown St. Louis—a plan that included Maurice and the three children.

On the college's short application form, she expressed regret she had dropped out of high school but pride that she had attained her GED in 1997. "My second accomplishment and the one I am most proud of," she wrote, "would be that for the past six years I have raised three wonderful and beautiful children on my own. Even with some struggles of everyday life, I pulled through and taken care of them in the best way possible. Now I am ready to give them and myself a better life and go for the career I want and need to succeed in my life."

Amanda inquired about housing and made plans to send the kids to a daycare operated by Maurice's half-sister there. With plans to study hospitality and tourism, she dreamed of becoming a travel agent—maybe moving to Las Vegas—and hoped her boyfriend might be inspired to complete a high school diploma program, maybe even take some college courses. Amanda longed for the things she knew made happy families happy: a sense of stability that comes with a steady and reliable partner and enough money to pay the bills with a little left over for some fun.

But the scope of Maurice's vision seemed more limited. He was willing to stay the course until he became bored or something better came along.

Amanda told friends she liked Maurice's smooth way of talking and good looks.

Their sex life, she said, was amazing.

Chapter Four

As Amanda left the treatment room that held her older son's body, her eyes met those of Christopher's father. He was on his way to see his dead son. Amanda and Greg Hamm did not speak.

Greg, along with the fathers of Austin and Kyleigh, arrived at the hospital after the boys had died. He received his call about the accident from one of Amanda's relatives just after he got off work at a retail store in Bloomington. He picked up his girlfriend and drove to the Clinton hospital.

Amanda's adoptive father, Mark Walston, took Christopher's father to a police officer who was not yet willing to answer questions about the boy's condition. That's when Walston broke the news to Hamm that Christopher and his brother had both died. Hamm went outside for some air and to collect his thoughts before seeing Christopher.

Austin's father, Craig Brown, was at his Bloomington home when he received a cell phone call from Amanda. At first it was difficult to understand what she was saying. He asked her to slow down.

"Get your ass over here right fucking now," Amanda finally told him, out of patience with his inability to comprehend the urgency.

Brown called the hospital but, like other family members, could get no information. Then he called his mother. She picked him up and drove to the hospital. When they arrived, hospital staffers could not let Brown see Austin. Medical efforts to save the child were still underway.

As Brown approached Amanda, she reached out to hug him.

"Get away from me," he said, pushing her back. "I don't want to talk to you." Then he saw Maurice in the hallway.

"Keep him away from me," Brown advised Amanda.

Amanda defended her boyfriend. "It's not his fault. It was an accident," she answered.

Hostility from the boys' fathers was not surprising to Amanda. Given her history with the men, she expected nothing else.

At about 8:15, Amanda reached Kyleigh's father at the Dugout Bar in Clinton where he was bartending. Shane Senters caught a ride to the hospital with a friend.

Maurice approached Senters in the emergency room, telling him "I'm sorry," then walked away without offering any information about what had happened. Eventually Senters learned something had occurred at the lake, but he didn't know how his daughter was involved. A doctor gathered him with other relatives of all three children in the chapel where he told them "the good news" that Kyleigh was being airlifted to Peoria. He also shared the heartbreaking news that the boys had died.

Senters and Amanda were escorted to the treatment room where Kyleigh was awaiting transport to Peoria. Amanda was silent. Senters wanted to know his daughter's chances, a question the doctor did not answer. It was too soon for predictions and the chances too slim.

As dusk gave way to dark at Clinton Lake, two state conservation department officers stood on the boat ramp, curious there was no sign of a boat trailer connected to the submerged vehicle. A quizzical, if not suspicious circumstance, thought Illinois Department of Natural Resources Sergeant Duane Pitchford.

His mounting skepticism about the circumstances surrounding the drownings centered on the surface of the boat ramp itself. It had been resurfaced a few years earlier with a deeply grooved texture that provided more traction, making mishaps less frequent.

Pitchford relayed his concerns in a call to DeWitt County Sheriff Roger Massey, who was at the hospital. The sheriff agreed to ask an Illinois State Police crime scene supervisor who lived in Clinton to go to the lake. While he was waiting for the crime scene worker and a dive team from nearby Decatur to help remove the car from the water, Pitchford recorded the water temperature at the dock. It was 78 degrees Fahrenheit at a depth of two feet.

With the help of divers, Detective Hawn determined the rear of the vehicle was 26.6 feet from the water's edge. As the car was pulled from the lake, the passenger side rear door swung open. Toys, dolls, diapers and young Christopher's favorite St. Louis Cardinals baseball cap spilled out into the lake and floated toward a nearby cove.

An examination of the car by police found all four doors unlocked and easily opened.

The front passenger window was completely down. The ignition was in the "on" position. The gear shift on the steering column was in "reverse." Every seat belt was unbuckled.

With the car on its way to storage at the sheriff's department as evidence, the road leading to the boat ramp was closed to the public. It had taken Pitchford 27 minutes to form his opinion that the site was potentially a crime scene.

As word of the tragedy spread, the scene outside the hospital grew more chaotic. Stressed firefighters and other first responders gathered in the parking lot for a much-needed break from the emotional powder keg inside. Their faces reflected the distress and disbelief that two of the three children could not be saved.

The Clinton fire chief hadn't been to the lake and assumed, like many others, that there had been a boating accident—an inaccurate conclusion he provided reporters who had begun to arrive at the hospital.

Unlike Maurice, Amanda was part of a family with deep roots in the community going back several generations. Hundreds of people were connected in some way to her, her family and her children. Such kinship made it impossible to stay separated from the massive tragedy that had struck the small town; what affected one, affected all. It even extended into how the sheriff would handle the investigation. After all, almost all his employees worked closely with Amanda's mother in her role as a secretary in the county prosecutor's office. That connection, along with the added resources the state had to offer, was part of why he asked the state police to send investigators to the hospital.

Sergeant Ben Halloran and Trooper Val Panizo were assigned to the case.

Thirty minutes after the two boys were pronounced dead, Sheriff Massey met with Maurice in the hospital's admissions office.

The trip to the lake was a spur of the moment idea for some "quality family time," Maurice told Massey. Maurice said he parked the car on the boat ramp—8 to 10 feet from the water—before everyone got out for about 45 minutes of playtime near the dock and water.

When they decided to leave, he said, the children were buckled in the rear seat. He put the car in reverse, the vehicle went backwards for several inches, then lurched forward into the water. The tires were spinning.

As the car floated further into the lake, Maurice unsuccessfully tried to escape through a window but then managed to open the driver's door. Amanda "popped up" in the water near him. He wasn't sure how she had exited the car.

Amanda waded through the 6 to 7 feet of water at the front of the car towards the pay phone on the shore to summon help. Unable to open the rear door of the car to rescue the kids, Maurice followed her.

Massey's interview was interrupted by family members wanting to ask Maurice their own questions. When Massey and Maurice resumed their discussion in the chapel 45 minutes later, the sheriff's questions were more pointed.

Why, Massey asked, did the two adults not return to the water to try to save the children?

"I did everything I could for those kids," Maurice responded. Massey pressed Maurice about his claim that there was no conversation between him and Amanda as the car went into the water and the children were not scared or screaming. Maurice stood by his earlier account.

Maurice said he applied the brakes but the car wouldn't stop its slide into the lake. When he got his car door open, the water was up to his ribs. As he tried to leave the car, his left foot was momentarily stuck on the edge of the door frame.

Massey asked Maurice about drug use. He admitted he and Amanda had smoked marijuana the previous evening when they shared a 20-dollar bag he had purchased but said they had used no drugs that day.

Massey would question Maurice four more times over the next 23 days.

At 1:20 a.m., state police investigators conducted their first interview with Amanda.

Her story started at the beginning of the dreadful day, with the boys going to school and Kyleigh to the babysitter. The day ended with the car parked 4 to 5 feet from the water on the boat ramp, she said, because initially the plan was to look at the water but not leave the car.

After playing on the dock, Amanda took Christopher to an outdoor toilet in the parking lot, up the embankment from the lake. The child ended up relieving himself outside, however, after deeming the toilet "too gross to use."

Amanda's version of the scene inside the car differed from her boyfriend's as she recalled the horrible frustration of trying to grab the youngest child.

She screamed as the car went deeper in the water, she said. She reached behind her to try to free Kyleigh from her car seat but didn't know if she had succeeded. The seat wasn't properly anchored to the car, she said, because of a broken latch.

"Mommy, Mommy, Mommy," were the words Hamm heard from her children as she went out her window.

Looking back from the boat ramp at the submerged car, Amanda could see her children's faces looking at her through the back window of the car as it filled with water. That memory seemed to wash over her as she told her story to the state police detectives. She had to pause.

Laying his suspicions on the table, Panizo suggested to Amanda the drownings may have been intentional.

"I would never do anything like that to my kids," Amanda told the detective.

Drugs and alcohol did not play a part in the accident, said Amanda, rebuffing Halloran's thought that maybe Maurice lost control of the car because he was in a marijuana haze.

"I feel it was a freak accident," she said. "It could have happened to anyone. It had nothing to do with alcohol or drugs."

Police weren't so sure. After the two interviews, they felt confident Maurice was behind the wheel when the car went into the lake and there was a good chance he was under the influence of marijuana. They charged him with driving under the influence of drugs and with driving on a suspended license.

Maurice agreed to provide urine and blood samples for testing. As he was being escorted by Hawn to the hospital's emergency room to collect the specimens, Maurice passed Amanda in the hallway. Hawn later said he overheard her whisper in her boyfriend's ear: "Don't worry. Stay strong."

Even before the two boys died, it was clear people in law enforcement and on the medical team were having doubts about reasons offered by Maurice and Amanda about why the children couldn't be saved. Viewed through the prism of these suspicions, it was highly improbable that the pair's denial of any intention to harm the children would be accepted.

Despite urging from her family to leave for the Peoria hospital where her daughter was being treated, Amanda stayed behind for about an hour to be with Maurice. He was being detained at the sheriff's department while officers processed the traffic citations.

Everyone clung to the hope that Kyleigh, the little girl everyone loved to adore, might survive. Her sweet nature was reflected in the warmth of her big brown eyes. Austin and Christopher were devoted to their little sister and looked out for her at home and on the playground. Kyleigh also was Maurice's favorite, the child he was gentle with during playtime but not so interested in when it came to routine childcare duties. Even so, Amanda had floated the idea of Maurice adopting her. Maurice didn't reject the idea but believed it was unlikely. Amanda's mother—Kyleigh's grandmother—would strongly object, Maurice believed.

Amanda's mother and her fiancé were the first in a caravan of people that left Clinton for the Peoria hospital to be at Kyleigh's bedside. Lindy Powers had made a quick trip home to pick up clothes for him and Ann and drop off a bag of Amanda's wet clothing he had been handed as he left the hospital. But the bag went back to Powers' car after the coroner called and said he wanted the clothing turned over to him.

The highway between Clinton and Peoria was shrouded in fog, making the trip both treacherous and even more agonizing. The sedatives given to Ann at the Clinton hospital left her in a fog of her own that would rob her of much of her memory about the trip.

Amanda's adoptive father took Amanda to be with Kyleigh. Maurice's departure was delayed by police who had more questions for him after he was booked and released on the driving under the influence charge.

Chances that Kyleigh could overcome the time underwater were nearly nonexistent. But her faint heartbeat gave hope to a desperate, grieving crowd that lined the hallway and waiting room in the Saint Francis Medical Center pediatric intensive care unit. Only immediate family and the closest of friends were allowed into Kyleigh's room. Others stayed nearby to lend support and perhaps a chance to see the little girl one last time.

The prognosis was extremely grim, a minister told family members when they entered the unit reserved for the youngest and sickest.

A portion of Amanda's focus was still on her boyfriend. Several times she borrowed a cell phone from Lindy to call Maurice. Each time she was told by police that he was in an interview, a situation that worried her. Could he be held in jail for the DUI? Eager for his emotional support, she left messages urging him to get to Peoria as soon as possible.

Mark Walston's parents drove Maurice, not arriving until 9:30 a.m. Maurice was openly affectionate towards Amanda in a way that did not go unnoticed by family members as they held their vigil for Kyleigh.

As the morning wore on, her condition worsened. Then the difficult decision was made to disconnect her from life support. Maurice joined the family for final good-byes. Amanda and Ann took turns holding Kyleigh until she took her last breath at 2:05 p.m. in her mother's arms.

Chapter Five

Turbulence that had erupted inside the Peoria hospital followed the family to Ann's home. Relatives and neighbors comforted Ann and Lindy at the door as they flowed into the bi-level house. Missing from the crowd were Maurice and Amanda. They had walked to a convenience store six blocks away for cigarettes.

When they returned, they disappeared again, this time into the bathroom where sounds heard outside the door told people they were showering together.

"The place was full of people. Just lost three kids and they were in that shower and you could hear them," Lindy told a private investigator who interviewed him later about the evening. "I thought that was very odd. Very odd."

With little concern for sleep for themselves or those involved in the deaths, investigators had gone looking for Amanda and Maurice at 9 p.m. to conduct another round of questioning. Halloran, a 14-year veteran with the state police, teamed up with Hawn, a county officer for 10 years, to conduct the follow-up. When they found them at Ann's home, the couple agreed to cooperate. They borrowed Amanda's mother's car for the five-minute drive to the sheriff's office.

Amanda and Maurice were placed in separate rooms at the sheriff's office.

When Halloran and Illinois State Police Special Agent Troy Phillips walked into the interview room, Amanda was lying on a couch, obviously distraught. She had vomited and asked to go to the bathroom.

Once she was settled, Phillips offered his condolences to Amanda. She was not in custody, he told her, and free to leave at any time. Amanda agreed to talk.

First to be addressed by investigators was new information Massey had received in a phone call from a woman who claimed she had been at the lake with her daughter, hoping to see deer, when a car driven by a black man sped past her on the road leading to the ramp. A small boy about three years old was standing in the backseat looking over the driver's shoulder, she said.

Massey had developed a new theory based on the phone call:

Perhaps Amanda was dropped off at the top of the hill, meaning she wasn't in the car when it rolled into the water—all part of a premeditated plan to kill the kids.

Phillips asked Amanda if she was lying down in the car as it went down the road to the boat launch. And did she see any other vehicles in the area?

Amanda insisted she was sitting up in the front seat. The only vehicle she recalled seeing was a police car on Route 10 near the turnoff to the lake. The cop was conducting a traffic stop, a detail later confirmed by Massey.

The responses Amanda gave to investigators' queries did not vary substantially from what she had told them earlier at the hospital, but she expanded on several details. After they parked on the ramp, Christopher's baseball hat flew into the water. Amanda took off all her clothes and waded into the water to retrieve it.

The chill of the water kept her from going too far into the lake before she gave up the effort, she said. When Austin announced he was tired and ready to go home, the three children climbed into the back seat for the ride home.

With the car so close to the water, Amanda said she tried to direct her boyfriend on the best way to back up the ramp: left foot on the brake and right foot on the gas. She believed he moved the gear shift into reverse as he stepped on the gas.

She told detectives the car slid quickly into the lake, water slapping against her face through the open car window. She told the children to unbuckle their seat belts.

Panic set in. "I was in shock. I didn't know what to do," she said.

Amanda recalled Maurice leaving the car before her. She swam, then waded, to the shore to call 911, with cries of "Help me, help me Mommy" echoing behind her.

The officers told Amanda discrepancies had begun to emerge between her recollections now and what she had told others, that what she was saying didn't line up with the physical evidence, that there were doubts a car placed in reverse gear would spin its wheels and go forward into the lake.

Amanda became upset with the insinuation that she was lying and had contributed to the deaths of her children. "I can't believe you are accusing me of killing my kids. I loved them and would never do anything to harm them," Amanda pushed back.

Love was not the issue for the detectives; the question was why everything possible hadn't been done to save the kids.

Shortly before 11 p.m., Amanda asked to end the interview.

"I want to go home. I've got to get out of here. I want an attorney," she said.

The detective explained that her request for a lawyer meant the interview was over. As they stood to leave the room, Amanda began screaming. "Wait. I didn't mean it! I want to talk to you," she said.

The only way the interview could continue was if she specifically asked to speak with police, Halloran told Amanda.

"Please help me, I want to talk with you, I don't want an attorney.... Please help me," Amanda pleaded.

Halloran and Phillips stepped into the hallway to discuss the situation. Amanda opened the door, yelling to the detectives, "I'm begging you please, please talk to me. I don't want an attorney."

Any worry Amanda might have had about wading into the treacherous depths of investigators' incriminating questions was replaced by a determination to make sure they understood this was a tragic accident and nothing more.

The detectives decided they could resume the interview because Hamm had reinitiated contact. But she would have to sign a voluntary statement acknowledging her constitutional rights, including the right to have a lawyer present during questioning.

"I requested a lawyer but decide to go on and talk w/o one present," she wrote on the form. "After requesting an attorney, I requested to speak with Sgt. Halloran and Agent Phillips w/o attorney. I made an effort to talk alone with officer w/o an attorney. It wasn't going to happen and I plead with them."

The interview went on with Massey taking over for Phillips.

The investigator had Amanda start from the beginning with her 8 a.m. shift as a waitress and ending with her spot in the passenger seat of a car parked on a boat ramp 12 hours later. The police team paid close attention to every detail, checking for more potential discrepancies.

When asked about efforts she made to get the children out of car, she admitted her attempts fell short.

"I tried to get them out. I could have tried harder," she said. "I didn't know what to do."

She said it was overwhelming fear and a panic over her inability to save the children that sent her rushing to the pay phone for help.

Investigators dug deeper into the relationship between Amanda and Maurice. Surely there was something more—something beyond mere incompetence—that kept two adults from pulling three young children from the car.

Was there a dark and sinister motive they were missing?

There was infidelity on Maurice's part, Amanda disclosed, but the affection he showed for her and the children seemed genuine.

"I don't believe he didn't care for them kids. I know he cared about them kids. I thought he loved my kids. I thought he loved me," she said, struggling to make officers fathom a complicated relationship that fell well below their standard of what a family should be.

The three-hour interview wrapped up with questions about whether the car was in reverse when Maurice pressed his foot on the accelerator. There was no talk about the gear, Amanda said. She just assumed it was in reverse. She repeated how she told Maurice to cover the brake pedal as he stepped on the gas.

Meanwhile in the conference room just down the hall, Maurice was asked to sign a Miranda form before the first question was posed by ISP Sgt. Greg Lindemulder and Panizo.

Maurice initially seemed confused about the location of the boat ramp. Detectives clarified the boat access was at Clinton Lake and not nearby Weldon Springs, a state park with a much smaller body of water.

Maurice explained how the car went into the water: With his foot on the brake, he put the car in reverse and hit the accelerator. The car jerked backwards and the tires were spinning as the car moved forward into the water.

What happened then, investigators wanted to know. Maurice said he was unable to roll down his window all the way, so he exited through the driver's side door with lake water about halfway up the door. His left foot became stuck in the door, forcing him to maneuver on one foot. He tried the rear door but it wouldn't open.

He said after Amanda headed for shore, his attempt to dive under the water was thwarted by the car's movement. Water was up to his neck when he made a second and final attempt to open the car doors.

"I can't get them out," Maurice said he yelled to his girlfriend.

Amanda's loud, hysterical conversation with the 911 dispatcher made its way down the hill to the water where Maurice was worried she was failing to communicate critical information needed to summon help. He ran up the hill, took the phone and clarified their location to the dispatcher. Then the call ended.

Amanda then tried to contact her mother, but the call wouldn't go through on the pay phone.

Parts of Maurice's account troubled detectives. Why, for example, was his left rather than his right foot caught in the door? Using a chair to demonstrate, Lindemulder pointed out that a person usually steps out of a car with his left foot and thus his right foot would be last to leave the vehicle, making it more likely to be hung up in the door. Maurice claimed he was unable to touch the lake bottom when he stepped from the car. To illustrate his actions, he grabbed the back of the chair, and spun out with his feet in the air.

The explanation and maneuver made no sense to police. They told Maurice as much. But that's the way it happened, Maurice insisted.

The agents jabbed more directly at the inconsistencies and detours they found between Maurice's version of events and what he and others had told police earlier. The lack of a solid timeline for certain segments of the day the children died and missing pieces of information—among them Amanda's naked trip into the lake for Christopher's hat—didn't add up, the agents informed Maurice.

Maurice switched the subject to his profound belief in God. Authorities who arrested and persecuted an innocent person would be punished by God, he said. Maurice considered himself such an innocent man.

At one point, Maurice began to recite the Lord's Prayer. His calm demeanor turned to involuntary shivers, profuse sweating and continuous yawns, detectives noted in their report.

The interview ended when Lindemulder, an 18-year veteran of the state police, confronted Maurice about his statement that he had managed to roll the driver's side car window down several inches, a statement at odds with the closed window found by police.

"Maybe I should have an attorney," Maurice told the agent, clearly more aware than his girlfriend of the potential legal handicaps a person faces in an interview room without an attorney.

After Lindemulder picked up his materials and left the room, Maurice asked Panizo to continue the interview so he could clear things up. Detectives read Maurice his constitutional rights a second time and had him sign a form confirming that he understood them.

Lindemulder returned to the room and asked Maurice what details he wanted to clear up. Maurice leaned forward, cupped his hands together and paused.

Maurice pointed to the investigators' notes.

"That's exactly how it happened."

The interview ended a second time. As Maurice stepped outside for a cigarette, detectives noticed two puddles of sweat on Maurice's chair.

Chapter Six

People were still awake—anxious and jarred—when Maurice and Amanda returned to her mother's house shortly after midnight.

Maurice asked if someone could make a pot of coffee. He slumped in a chair at the table. It seemed the gravity of the situation had settled on him.

"They're wanting to give me some serious time. They think I had something to do with it," Maurice told Amanda's family.

Ann's experience with the legal profession surfaced. She advised Maurice to be cautious in how he answered questions. Police could trick him, twist his words, she said.

Ann's advice rankled her sister, Kathy Clifton. She had suspicions about how the children had died. A few minutes later, when they were alone in a bedroom down the hallway, Clifton expressed her concerns to Ann.

Only Amanda seemed to offer comfort to Maurice.

"We need to talk," Maurice told Amanda. "We need to get our stories straight," he said, now worried that police tried to pit her against him in the separate interviews. It was a comment that upset everyone within hearing distance, one that would be resurrected many times in coming months as a footprint that led to guilt. Each time the remark was repeated to investigators, it weakened chances Maurice and Amanda could explain the deaths as an accident.

To test Maurice's truthfulness, Lindy Powers asked Maurice a question he already knew the answer for: Had Maurice been issued any traffic citations?

Still rattled from the tenor of the police interview, Maurice denied he had been arrested for any driving offenses.

"You're a liar," Powers challenged. The volume of the discussion was rising.

Clifton joined in, directing her skepticism towards Amanda. Why, she wondered, did the grandmother seem more traumatized than the mother who had just lost three children?

"They were *my* fucking kids," Amanda shot back at her aunt.

The interchange grew more intense, Maurice and Amanda feeling trapped by the relatives' insinuations that mirrored those raised by police hours earlier.

"We didn't do nothing wrong. I love my kids," Amanda shouted.

As the yelling match edged closer to a physical confrontation between weary and overwrought family members, Powers became concerned. He called 911, asking police to remove Maurice from the house. As officers arrived, Maurice and Amanda were walking out the back door.

Family members convinced Amanda to stay at the house. Police drove Maurice to the apartment he shared with Amanda.

The next day DeWitt County State's Attorney Jerry Johnson announced that because of the conflict of interest that existed with Amanda's mother working in his office, a special prosecutor would handle the driving offenses pending against Maurice. A soft-spoken man who didn't chase media attention, Johnson was not disappointed with the need to excuse himself from a matter he knew could explode into the most serious criminal case in county history.

On Sept. 4, the coroner confirmed that the boys were drowning victims. The same cause of death would be indicated for Kyleigh several days later.

In his public statements, Sheriff Massey offered nothing beyond the official autopsy results. His refusal to even imply that the coroner's report provided some conclusive answers raised more doubts among the media and public: It seemed clear authorities were far from convinced this was all an accident.

"We don't want to blow this up into something that it's not," Massey told a room full of reporters from multiple media markets, including Chicago. "But on the other side, we've got three children who are dead. None of us knows exactly what happened."

For the community, the uncommon deaths of three young children were agonizing. A 10-on-the-Richter-Scale earthquake couldn't be more traumatizing. Everyone needed help.

Counselors met with emergency workers still struggling with the aftermath of the call that ended so badly. Students at the elementary school where Christopher was a first grader and Austin attended pre-school had specially trained grown-ups they could talk to about the deaths of their classmates. Backpacks went home from school containing letters to parents outlining tips on how to help grieving youngsters.

The boat ramp was transformed into a makeshift memorial. A cross, along with a framed photo of Christopher in his baseball uniform, marked the spot of the tragedy. People visited the ramp to try to wrap their minds around what had happened there. Usually they left saddened, with more questions than answers.

Mostly, people tried to understand why Maurice and Amanda didn't do what they felt certain they personally would have done in a similar situation: Die, if necessary, to save the children.

The same day the coroner disclosed his findings, Amanda agreed to return to the boat ramp with Hawn and Halloran for a third round of questions, again without an attorney to look after her interests. Public access to the area was blocked as police videotaped the interview.

Detectives began by playing a recording of the 911 call made by Amanda as her children were drowning. Amanda's first words on the call were largely unintelligible.

"What's going on?" the dispatcher asked.

"My kids are in the car! The car is going into the lake. I need help!"

"Ma'am, you need to calm down for just a minute. I can't understand a word you're saying."

"My kids are in my car. My car is in the fuckin' lake!"

"Okay. Your, your kids are underneath the car?"

"No. My kids are in the car!"

"Are in the car?"

"Yes, and my car is in the lake!"

"Is the car moving or what—you need to calm down for just a second. I need to know what's goin' on."

Maurice had taken the phone from Amanda.

"Ma'am, we're down here at the lake right now."

"Uh-huh."

"We're at the—we are at..."

Maurice's words were away from the phone and muffled. The dispatcher probed.

"Okay. But what's wrong? What's wrong? I can't understand what she's saying."

"Huh? What are you sayin', ma'am? Talk to me, lady."

"What's wrong with her kids?"

"The kids are in the water in the car drowning."

"Oh shoot. It's at 674 1375 East. Is that where it's at?" The dispatcher was checking the location of the pay phone with a colleague.

"I don't know," Maurice said. "You gotta have a trace on this damn phone."

"Kids trapped in the lake in a car." The dispatcher was sending help. Amanda was back on the phone.

"West side access."

"It's the west side access?"

"Yes! Hurry. Please hurry. My kids are in my car drowning. Please hurry."

"Okay, ma'am. We've got somebody on the way. I need—"

"I need help. I need help."

"How many kids are in the car?"

"Three."

"There's three? How old are they?"

"Six. Six, three and one. Oh my God."

"Okay. Please. You need to calm down. Okay."

"Oh my God. My kids!"

Maurice reclaimed the phone.

"Do you have all the information you need?"

"No. I need you—they're at the west side access. I'm gonna keep someone on the line 'til we get someone there, okay? So I can make sure they find it."

"You don't know where we at? I just told you!"

"You're at west side access, right?"

"Yes, west side access."

"Is the, is the car all the way in the water? I mean, is it covering in the water?"

"Yes."

Hawn shut off the tape recorder. Amanda's hands covered her face. She walked toward the lake. "It's not wet. It's not wet," she said, looking at the ramp's dry, ridged surface.

Her fresh account of what had happened, starting with Maurice's decision to park four to six feet from the water, was substantially the same as what she had said in her two previous conversations with police.

When it was time to leave the ramp that fateful day, she volunteered, Maurice became a bit agitated when she told him how to back the car away from the lake. "I know. I know," Maurice told his girlfriend, before he put the car in gear and shouted "hold on" to the three young occupants in the back seat.

Halloran and Hawn asked Amanda to demonstrate the speed at which the car rolled into the water. Her gait down the ramp was characterized as "a run but not a sprint" in a report of the interview written later by police.

"We immediately rolled into the water." Maurice was saying "Oh my God, oh my God," she said.

Amanda couldn't remember whether she escaped through a door or a window but knew it was on the driver's side of the car. She assumed Maurice was working to free her kids. "He told me later that's what he was doing," she said.

She recalled briefly stopping to look back as she ran to call for help. Amanda said Maurice yelled to her, "What the hell are you doing?" The children's faces were visible in the back window. She heard their screams for help.

When rescuers arrived, Maurice held Amanda back from the water, she recalled.

"I told him over and over again to get the fuck off me. He kept holding me."

The next day, Sept. 5, Maurice also agreed to accompany police to the boat ramp to answer questions. Maurice and five policemen arrived at 1 p.m. for the videotaped session.

Halloran wanted to know whether Maurice had been nervous about backing the car up the ramp that day.

No, he said. Speaking in calm, measured tones, Maurice said he had safely managed the same maneuver many times on ramps along the Mississippi River in St. Louis. He said he told Amanda, "It would be fucked up for the car to slip into the water."

Maurice again described how he looked over his shoulder and put the car in gear—he assumed it was in reverse—and punched the accelerator. Halloran wanted more details, pointing out how the pavement on the ramp was dry, that there was no sign of tread marks left by spinning wheels just a few days earlier.

A fretful melancholy seemed to grip Maurice as he didn't seem to grasp Halloran's explanation that the car's front wheel drive mechanism would cause the front, rather than the back, tires to spin.

"I'm not sure of all the technicalities, actually. I'm not sure if the rear tires spin," Maurice responded.

Halloran made his point for the camera.

"I would like to document there is no evidence to support tires spinning out here. That's why I brought that up, OK? Because we have a conflict of statements here, as I pointed out earlier, we need to get the correct one, the way things happened, OK? "

Maurice nodded. The car's braking system was next for scrutiny.

"Were the brakes able to hold the vehicle?" Halloran asked.

"Some, but today is a totally different day from that day. That day was a gloomy day. It was misty, had been raining prior to that for a couple days," said Maurice.

Maurice described how he tried to lower the window in the driver's door and, failing at that, opened the door itself.

"I was panicking. I was terrified, you know, and I was just using my instincts to try to find the best way to get those kids out of the water and back to safety."

Maurice said it took four or five tries before he could push his door open as the car rolled into the lake. And after it closed behind him, he was unable to open either door on the driver's side of the car.

Halloran asked what the kids were doing at that point. "They were trying to…" Maurice paused, looking toward the sky. "Trying to get air as much as possible because the water was still rising." He said he saw Kyleigh's face disappear as water filled the car's back seat.

Maurice said he couldn't remember where he and Amanda were standing when the first squad car arrived or how long it took to run from one spot to another in the sequence of events.

The detectives asked Maurice why his voice was heard at the beginning of the 911 call, a fact at odds with Maurice's earlier assertion that he was in the water, trying to save the kids, when Amanda began screaming into the phone. Maurice was unsure whether minutes or seconds had elapsed before he was at his girlfriend's side.

He said he consoled Amanda near the dumpster. "You know, talking to her, asking her to let them do their job. They didn't need any obstruction at the time."

There was one last point Halloran wanted to review.

"I'd like you to show me again the front of the car, where you were, where the car initially started from when you got ready to leave and back up the ramp."

A battery on the video camera went dead as Halloran asked another question.

But now, police had both Maurice and Amanda on tape, describing what had occurred. And nothing had erased their opinion that this surely was not an accident.

Now they sought proof that these two people who had lived quietly, nearly unnoticed on the fringe of society were driven to murder three innocent children who meant everything to their mother.

Chapter Seven

The longer and deeper the mystery of the deaths churned, the wider the audience grew for tidbits of news. Grecian Gardens, the restaurant where Amanda and Maurice worked, attracted reporters from across the United States. Townspeople were close to awestruck when CNN came to their community, seeking out those willing to convey their anxiety and sadness to a camera.

"As a town, we feel like we're under the microscope," a restaurant manager told one reporter. Overall, national media coverage of the death case with its many unanswered questions was not the kind of attention Clinton was hoping to attract.

DeWitt County was proud of its history, especially long-ago ties to a young lawyer who traveled the 8th Judicial Circuit, representing clients in Clinton. His talents caught the attention of the new Republican Party, and in 1860, Abraham Lincoln was elected the 16th president of the United States. It's commonly believed that it was during a debate about two years earlier on Clinton's town square Lincoln first suggested it was possible to "fool all of the people some of the time."

Settled by two land speculators in 1835, the town and county were named in honor of New York Governor DeWitt Clinton. The cross-country expansion of railroads transformed the frontier community into a bustling "railroad town" with shops and new homes.

Farming was a mainstay for the local economy. But a mix of local manufacturing and retail business emerged as testament to the hard work of community leaders from each generation, determined to see the town prosper. Like many small communities, Clinton's growth slowly eased away from the central business district, leaving empty storefronts where Ben Franklin and Woolworth stores once met everyone's needs.

When the town landed a Revere Copper and Brass plant in 1950, the potential for hundreds of steady jobs making copper-clad pots was considered an economic development triumph. Not long after, Wal-Mart and McDonald's appeared on the town's western edge once considered part of the rural landscape.

Plans by Illinois Power Co. to build a nuclear power plant in 1974 were welcomed by residents and government officials alike. The boon from thousands of construction jobs, millions in new property tax revenue and the creation of a 5,000-acre lake held economic promise for generations to come. The lake and its surrounding recreational area attracted camping, boating and fishing enthusiasts from hours away. People who grew up in DeWitt County and never learned to swim boarded newly-purchased boats.

Hundreds of nuclear power professionals, many of them retired military, set down fresh roots in DeWitt County. Meanwhile many Clinton residents, particularly those with office skills and high school graduates willing to learn a new trade, found steady employment at the plant, too.

Even so, DeWitt County's demographics changed little over the years. A recent census put its population at 16,800. Only one half of one percent were black. Mixed race couples were rare and raised eyebrows among longtime residents.

For many of its residents, DeWitt County was the first and last place they would ever live.

Connections between neighbors were strong, almost family-like. People counted on each other when things were tough, just as they celebrated the good times together. They tended to think the best of someone, extending the benefit of the doubt, taking into account where they came from, leaving harsh judgments to strangers.

In short, it took an awful lot for people to turn against a neighbor.

Some diners at Grecian Gardens bristled as reporters sought feedback on Sheriff Massey's suggestion that the incident was somehow similar to the Susan Smith case in South Carolina eight years earlier. Smith had been convicted of strapping her two young sons into their car seats and then rolling the car into a lake, drowning them. Wait until all the facts are in, Clinton residents told the media.

But in other coffee shops across town, hints of unspoken skepticism subtly crept into conversations. How, the question was quietly being asked, could three children drown in a car settled in just four feet of water while two adults stood on the shore?

"I would die trying to save my children" steadily grew the refrain on front porches, in shops and on the online comment boards attached to news stories about the drownings.

Feeling pressure from the public and the media, Amanda's family prepared a statement. "There are no words to fully express the pain we are currently experiencing," it read. "The love within our family, our faith in God and the generous support of our friends and community will pull us through this."

The statement was distributed by Rev. Billy Bell, pastor of the church the children attended with Amanda's adopted father and his wife. Family members requested privacy while vowing to help authorities.

"Our family is in a period of mourning and would appreciate being allowed to grieve outside the glare of the media," the statement continued. "Despite gossip and rumors on the street, let it be known that all members of our family are cooperating completely and fully with the ongoing investigation."

Memorial funds were established at local banks. Amanda's co-workers hosted a dinner at Grecian Gardens to raise money for the family.

Planning the children's funeral held moments of discord. To avoid confrontations with the children's three fathers, Maurice would not be allowed to attend the visitation or funeral.

Members of Maurice's family, who had driven 150 miles to Clinton when they learned the news from his father, were also politely told they should not stay for the services. They left behind a monetary donation with their condolences before returning to St. Louis.

The night before the funeral on Sept. 8, hundreds of mourners stood for hours at the church, waiting to pay their respects. Teachers, friends, people who had worked or spent time with the children's parents—sometimes in church, sometimes in a bar—waited alongside courthouse employees who knew Ann Danison.

Young neighbors and classmates, uncomfortable with the sight of their friends in three open white caskets filled with teddy bears and flowers, leaned against their parents as the line crept towards the front of the church.

A table in the entryway was covered with photographs, laying out the love and joys of the children's lives. A book recorded the many names of those who came to express their sorrow.

Amanda occasionally stepped outside to get some fresh air and talk with visitors in the parking lot. She also spoke on a cell phone with Maurice. He was in Bloomington.

The next day, six days after the car had slid into the lake, two black hearses waited outside the church for the private funeral to end. Lacking an invitation, reporters and camera crews stood on a lawn across from the church. Negative remarks were shouted by some mourners on their way into the church, letting the media know there were those who considered death and grief a private matter, not something to be shared with the outside world or, certainly, exploited.

The watching reporters were keenly aware that at any moment, the deaths could be classified as something more than an accident. That would make everything that happened along the way highly relevant, a justification for their unwelcome presence.

The funeral procession slowly drove the two miles to a cemetery on the north edge of town. Mourners walked the short distance from the road to the open graves where the siblings would be laid to rest side by side. Amanda clutched a Bible and sobbed openly during the graveside ceremony.

While the minister said some prayers, two of Amanda's friends yelled at reporters and photographers who watched the scene from across the road. After a few minutes, the media packed up, disinclined to disrupt the graveside service's final moments. It ended just as the mid-day sun was raising the temperature to a summertime level.

Maurice stayed at his father's home in Bloomington during the funeral. Meanwhile, legal wheels began to revolve.

Roger Simpson, an experienced attorney and former state's attorney from neighboring Piatt County, was named special prosecutor in the case by DeWitt County Judge Stephen Peters. Simpson's job would be to review material gathered by police, then determine if criminal charges should be filed against anyone. He also advised investigators on how to collect information. Among his first directives: Record all interviews with Amanda and Maurice on both audio and videotape.

With their final goodbyes to the children behind them, family members still grappled with details of the drownings that made no sense to them.

The day after the funeral, Ann confronted her daughter. Why, she wondered, had Maurice parked on the boat ramp? Amanda had no better answer for her mother than she had offered police.

"I don't know. That's just where he wanted to park."

The conversation grew more intense when Ann forced Amanda to admit that her relationship with Maurice remained intact. Wiretaps the family had allowed police to place on their phones confirmed the contact, Ann told her.

Amanda's refusal to break ties with Maurice infuriated her family and reinforced growing doubts about her version of events. Ann wanted her daughter out of the house. Amanda caught a ride back to Bloomington with Craig Brown and his girlfriend Jill Peavler, Amanda's close friend.

Later that day, Ann called Detective Hawn, asking whether he'd meet with her, several family members and Rev. Bell. They had doubts and frustrations to share and wanted to see what police would be willing to tell them. Eager for any new information from the family, Hawn quickly agreed to come to Ann's home.

Hawn told the group he'd be unable to answer questions about the pending investigation. What the family shared with him, however, would help fill in some blanks about Amanda and Maurice, now considered suspects in a criminal matter.

Ann shared Amanda's history of mental health and drug treatment. Information about Amanda's use of marijuana and cocaine was passed along by a cousin and by Christopher's father. The detective left the meeting confident Amanda's family wanted the truth, no matter where it led or whom it implicated. Their cooperation could be important assistance to law enforcement, he thought.

Two weeks had now passed since the drownings. Aware people craved information about the case, Sheriff Massey issued a statement, assuring anxious townspeople that investigators were working 12 and 18 hours a day on the case. "We're living and breathing it," it read. "We can't go out in public without hearing from people who are saying that nothing about this makes any sense."

He acknowledged the town's growing impatience.

"I understand that. If we're being this cautious, people don't see this in a typical investigation. But this is more intense than a normal case. There's nothing normal about this."

Massey revealed the probe now had the total attention of six state police and sheriff's department investigators.

Chapter Eight

Detectives were still short of what it would take to achieve critical mass and serious criminal charges. They were convinced, however, that one, maybe even both, survivors would lead them to that requisite particle of information.

No one who has watched even one episode of any TV police drama would believe it was a good idea for Amanda or Maurice to answer more questions from police without a lawyer at their side. But Amanda did just that on Sept. 10, a full week now after the deaths of her children.

Before setting up the interview, police contacted Richard Goff, a former DeWitt County state's attorney. He had been present when Amanda signed a written statement following the interview recorded at the lake. He declined to be formally involved unless she had retained him as her attorney. She hadn't.

Jill Peavler drove Amanda to the sheriff's department. Reservations police had about Peavler early on because of her friendship with Amanda weakened when she agreed to act as a confidential source, providing investigators whatever information she was able to collect from Amanda. The two women had been friends for several years. They had even shared the same boyfriend at one point in Craig Brown. His serious doubts about the version of events Amanda and Maurice were telling police impelled Peavler.

Halloran had two female state police detectives, Rebecca DeWitt Early and Cheryl Sims, with him for the third interrogation of Amanda. Again, she verbally agreed to speak without benefit of an attorney.

Halloran opened the conversation by telling Amanda authorities were fairly confident the deaths were the result of an intentional act.

"I understand that you are under a lot of pressure here," he said. "But from our investigation, we've been able to put together the 'who.' I'm talking about Christopher, Austin and Kyleigh. They're not coming back. They're buried in the ground. No matter what, Amanda, we know those three kids died because they drowned, Amanda. So we know the 'how' and the 'what' happened. But the big question—and the question you need to answer for yourself—is the way this occurred."

Agent Early would take on the role of a female friend, another woman Amanda could confide in, police hoped.

"What we need to figure out, what you need to do," Early said, "is start thinking about yourself now. This is all about Amanda right at this point." Early was trying to be soothing, encouraging Amanda to produce details that could benefit herself.

But Halloran hammered away again before Amanda could respond.

"Do you wish you could take this back? Do you wish you could take this all back and bring these three kids back to you again today?"

"Yes," Amanda answered. "I want my babies. I love my babies."

Halloran pressed forward, saying scientific evidence didn't support her statement that the car went into the water by accident.

"We've been out there. We've tested the car. We've done a full mechanical inspection. We know that car will drive up the ramp with the front tires submerged in the water. We know this car didn't go into the water immediately. That didn't happen that way." And, Halloran prodded, there's no evidence either Maurice or Amanda made much of an effort to pull the kids from the car.

Halloran paused, turning to Early.

"You need to figure out Amanda's life," she said. "You need to figure out where you're gonna go—okay?—and what you're gonna do next."

The media—everything from the local newspapers to CNN—would help define Amanda's future, Halloran added.

"Now, you're gonna leave here one way or the other. As a cold, calculated, murderous bitch that went out there with the intent to murder these three little kids because they were excess baggage, okay? Cold, calculated, heartless, murderous bitch. That's one end of the spectrum we're looking at, all right?"

Or, Halloran said, it could go another way.

"We've got a young mother in financial trouble, with a high amount of stress trying to raise three kids on her own."

The sympathetic narrative continued. The poor, single mother has a boyfriend, he said.

"And this boyfriend is very possessive. He's very controlling. And these kids are an obstacle to him and, I think, maybe he took advantage of this mother and persuaded her to do something she didn't want to do."

There it was: the suggestion that Amanda could be cajoled into doing anything that would hurt the three most precious people in her life. That upset Amanda.

"I loved my kids so much." Nothing, she said, could ever change that devotion. "No matter how much financial situation I had, no matter how much baggage I've had from my past, I would never hurt those kids."

If it wasn't money or family issues, Early wanted to know, then what went wrong on Sept. 2?

"Nothing went wrong," Amanda insisted. "I don't know what was going through his head because we weren't fighting or nothing."

Agent Sims joined the interrogation. "This is very serious. You've already been told that it's determined it wasn't an accident. This is your chance. We're not here to do anything to hurt you."

Then, as if a giant hour glass were about to run out of sand on Amanda's time to confess, Sims pressured her to look after her own interests.

"You are not gonna have a lot of time. That's why it's important. It's on your shoulders now to tell us what happened. How did this come about?"

"I have no idea," Amanda said. "I honestly don't know. "

Early said Amanda had no future unless she gave officers the truth. "Where do you think you're gonna be a year from now?"

"I want to go to school. I want to do everything that I've talked about—with my children."

"You think you're gonna have a life like that?" Early asked. "This is your time to talk about something that went severely wrong."

"I honestly don't know what went wrong," Amanda responded. "I wasn't in the driver's seat. How can I answer for someone who was driving? I don't know what went wrong. I've told you guys everything."

"No, no," Early interrupted. "And I'll tell you what. I'm not even gonna go there. Because if you want to sit in here and start saying more lies…"

"I thought that he had the car in reverse. If he didn't, I honestly don't know."

Their investigation, the detectives said, would move forward with or without Amanda's cooperation. It would be unwise, they repeated, for her to waste this chance to provide her side of things.

"Was this something you and Maurice had discussed?" Early asked.

"No. God." said Amanda. She seemed shocked by the direct accusation that she and Maurice had plotted the drownings.

"Is it something that happened at the last minute?"

"I don't know," said Amanda.

"I don't believe you, Amanda. I believe there was a decision made. What I want to know is who made that decision!"

"Nobody made no decision because nobody wanted to hurt my babies."

There had to be criminal intent, Early insisted, because there was no effort to save the kids.

"I was trying to get Kyleigh, and the water was comin' in so fast," Amanda said. "And the best thing I could think to do was call 911. And that's what I went and did."

Sims had grown impatient. "Amanda, it doesn't fit. You don't know what we have. You don't know who we've talked to. And you don't know the evidence that we have. It doesn't fit. I don't want to hear that anymore. It doesn't work."

Early again urged Amanda to protect herself because, after all, she was alone in this.

"If you think that you and Maurice—and you probably feel real tight right now—are gonna be together five years from now, you're nuts. It's not gonna happen. He's gonna be gone."

And Amanda, Early said, would be left to carry the blame and guilt for what happened to the children. "This is Amanda's choice 'cause Maurice isn't here. Your babies are dead."

The possibility of being prosecuted started to sink in for Amanda as the officers pressed her for details that fit their murder theory. "I mean, I need to get a lawyer and..."

Sims interrupted. "And if that's what you want to do, that's fine. And then we'll sit with him and talk to him—sit with you and the attorney."

"I think it's best if I have a lawyer present," Amanda repeated.

Halloran burst into the room. He had been watching through a one-way glass.

"That's your decision," he snapped. "This interview is done. We're not talking with you any more today. Today was truth time. You're requesting an attorney. We're gonna stop right now."

The 30-minute videotaped interview was over. But Amanda's fixation on trying to explain the tragedy to police remained. And investigators' determination to get a confession was even greater.

Chapter Nine

Police were satisfied the front-wheel drive Cutlass was mechanically capable of backing up the ramp. Now they scratched for proof Maurice and Amanda were the type of people capable of killing children. Detective Halloran, in particular, was on the lookout for evidence that Amanda was the cold, calculating, murderous bitch he had described to her, that Maurice was the controlling boyfriend who demanded sex and drugs and wished the children didn't exist.

As if the weight of crushing grief were not enough to bear, Amanda's family was also dealing with the growing public skepticism over whether the children's deaths were a freak accident. The family tried to hold tight to a trust that authorities would find the truth.

Hoping another face-to-face meeting would yield an update on the investigation, Amanda's mother met with Detective Hawn on Sept. 12. She was again disappointed when he declined to answer questions that nagged her. But when she thought to ask about what charges her daughter could face, Hawn responded. Child endangerment was a possibility. Maybe involuntary manslaughter. Maybe worse, he said.

"Child endangerment is not severe enough," Ann told Hawn. For the sake of her dead grandchildren, she stressed, she wanted the full truth.

Amanda and Maurice were still staying together at his father's home in Bloomington. They spent the evening of Sept. 16 talking about their relationship. When the conversation turned to recent histories with other partners, Maurice disclosed he had been with several other women in Clinton and made sexual advances towards her best friend and a cousin.

Amanda left the room, angry and hurt over her boyfriend's admissions—still more confirmation for her that men found her unworthy of a truly monogamous relationship. The timing of the confessions also incensed Amanda: Why would he share such horrific information when she was already reeling from the loss of her children?

Amanda shared her rage with Peavler who was detecting a definite change in her friend's attitude towards Maurice. Austin's father, Craig Brown, let police know Amanda had reached out to Peavler, his live-in girlfriend. Still acting as a police informant, Peavler eagerly picked up Amanda at the LaGrone family home. She believed Amanda now feared Maurice.

Amanda was willing to talk and shared her newly developed notion that Maurice had intended to kill the children—and her. Amanda was close to spelling out all her thoughts to Peavler and Brown but stopped just short, saying she wanted to save some details for a meeting she hoped to have the next day with Detective Hawn. She had another reason to go to Clinton—a 9 a.m. court hearing on a traffic citation she had received two months earlier for driving an uninsured car.

Peavler quickly relayed the striking new allegation to police and a plan was made for an early morning meeting. Amanda spent a restless night at her friends' home, finally giving up on sleep at 4 a.m.

So long before sunrise on Tuesday, Sept. 17, Peavler already had Amanda at the sheriff's department for her fourth meeting with police without a lawyer. Sheriff Massey, Halloran and Hawn were waiting. Amanda would first have to rescind her request for legal representation. Hawn asked her to speak up so the audio recorder could capture everything said. "I mean, we want this to be the last time," he said.

The detectives had decided they would let Amanda lead the conversation. She began by talking about her relationship with Maurice.

"Everything seemed really good at first," she said. "I'm not sure when things went bad. I'd always heard things about cheating. We were constantly arguing. Things between me and Maurice had gotten heated several times. It's hard to even talk about."

The heat produced more than angry words, she said. After an argument over attention she was receiving from a man she knew from a previous job, Maurice forced her to have sex. It was a violent encounter, she said, one that damaged her bladder.

Whenever Amanda's narrative swerved to negative things about Maurice—she thought he had a gun and may have been involved with gangs—Hawn steered her back to their relationship. She had more to offer. Maurice was jealous of Amanda's friends and wanted her all to himself. His behavior with the children left them frightened. Before bedtime, she said, "he'd go up there and act like he was a monster, make scary noises to them."

While Amanda's additional details were helpful, they weren't the specific thread that could tie the drownings to Maurice's jealousy and pranks. Life wasn't good, but not so bad that Maurice openly wished the children were somewhere else—or dead.

"He never came right out and said, you know, I wish the kids weren't here or anything. But body language and certain things that he'd say—he would get frustrated because the kids wouldn't go upstairs and play. The kids always wanted to be with me," Amanda continued.

The relationship was covered with a crust of hard feelings that seldom dissolved. Then more whispers of infidelity would thicken tensions in the apartment.

Shortly before Sept. 2, Amanda said, she was told Maurice had been with a specific woman, the latest in a series of rumors that he was chronically unfaithful. She was angry. The latest scuttlebutt "started a whole ball of fire," she said.

Maurice didn't react well.

"He was constantly questioning me, which made matters worse, and him telling me I was crazy, that I have some kind of mental disorder and I didn't know what the hell I was talking about. He made me feel like shit under his shoe."

She was ready to kick Maurice out after the latest accusations, but fear took over. At least once before she had thrown him out when stories came to her about two women. "And I took him back. I was always the one that went back."

Hawn helped Amanda distill her thoughts. "You liked having somebody to be with," he offered, "even if that somebody wasn't necessarily the right somebody."

"Yes."

"A little bit dependent on him and he probably fed on that. Being the manipulative and controlling person that he was, he liked having somebody that needed him there. Kind of gave him an ego boost."

Yes, maybe. But their arguments never included even a threat of violence, Amanda continued.

"He would sit there and say, you know, 'If you kick me out, you're never gonna see me again. You don't realize what you're losing. You're losing a good man. You know I've treated you good.' And I believed them things," she said, filling in more blanks.

The detectives tried to draw a small perimeter around the enmity leading to the events of Sept. 2.

The day before the drownings, Amanda said, Maurice had played one of his pranks on Christopher, holding a knife, pretending he was going to harm the boy.

"Did you confront him over that?" the sheriff wanted to know.

Amanda shook her head. "I was afraid for them and I was afraid for me."

Amanda didn't understand why Maurice seemed to enjoy scaring the kids. Now, since their deaths, the conflict between what constitutes a desirable family life and Maurice's cheating seemed to take on new meaning for Amanda. It was almost as if she had a new vantage point from which to view those weeks of turbulent conversations.

"I wanted a family," she said. "I wanted a husband. I wanted to make a good life for my kids. And I thought that he loved me. I thought that he loved the kids." But, she admitted, Maurice never expressed those same intentions and feelings. Now she believed her boyfriend's plans "were to use me for whatever he could get."

Even though Maurice said he supported the idea of moving to St. Louis and attending college there, Amanda doubted he would follow through. He was lazy and lacked ambition, she said. St. Louis was attractive to him only because he had family there. That meant there would be child care and other kinds of support.

They had driven to St. Louis to look for housing for two adults and three children. Yes, the move and managing a college schedule would be a financial and mental challenge, she said, "but I was willing to give my everything to do this for my children and for myself."

Meanwhile Amanda's family was worried about her prospects in St. Louis, a two-and-a-half-hour drive from Clinton. "They knew that I'd eventually, more than likely, end up on the streets because he was draining me financially, which I never told them how he was," Amanda said. "But they knew."

Her older son, Christopher, also understood what the move could mean. He'd miss his weekly overnights with Grandma Ann, his "Nonny." He instinctually feared losing the safety net she and his school represented.

In an unstable environment, these were important pieces of a 6-year-old's life.

Chapter Ten

A s the interview continued, Amanda finally admitted some of her arguments with Maurice had gotten physical, leaving bruises on her neck. But she had suffered through previous abusive relationships, she said, and felt confident she could cope through the bad times, even if the children were vulnerable.

Moving the timeline forward, Massey and Hawn gently prodded Amanda to tell them everything she could recall about Sept. 2. The investigators were eager to keep Amanda's focus on the connection between Maurice's aggressive nature and what took place at the lake— even if they were forming that link through their questions.

She remembered how her lingering distrust and disappointment over the attention Maurice gave other women added to her frustration at the end of what had been a long day at work. When she finally got home, she was silent. Maurice wanted to know why.

"It was like mind games," she told the detectives. "He was always like nitpickin' to start something. He was frustrated with me because I wouldn't talk to him." That tension followed the family to The Shack for dinner. "And he always felt like people were lookin' at him because he was black and felt like everyone was judging him because of how he looked."

Amanda's narrative continued. After dinner, Maurice didn't object to her idea about taking the kids to the lake. He drove. She gave directions.

After he turned off Route 10 onto the blacktop road leading to the boat ramp, Maurice started to drive too fast for Amanda's comfort. She asked him to slow down. "You worry too much," he said.

"I didn't know what to think," she told the investigators. "It scared me. And when he parked on the ramp, that scared me. I don't know why he parked there because I told him to park up by the pay phone and the dumpster. But he wanted to park there."

When the car stopped only feet from the water's edge, Maurice turned to Amanda. "So what are we gonna do? Just sit here?"

Amanda explained how she wanted to let the kids play and burn off some energy before bedtime. "Just let them have fun for a little bit."

Amanda said Maurice engaged the boys in a way that put more fear than fun in the outing with the same clueless disregard he sometimes exhibited at home. Maurice stood on the nearby dock and held Christopher, then Austin, upside down over the water. Christopher's baseball hat fell into the water. Maurice was able to retrieve it. It wasn't so wet that Christopher couldn't still wear it. Amanda summoned the children off the dock and took Austin up the hill to the bathroom. After less than an hour, the excursion began to wind down when Austin said he was tired and wanted to go home.

Their departure was delayed because Christopher's beloved ball cap had found its way into the water a second time. His mother stripped off all her clothes and waded into the water, but only a short distance. A childhood experience at that very location haunted her.

"A long time ago, when I was younger, my real father had taken me and his girlfriend's daughter boating," she remembered. "Well, he decided it would be funny to leave me and the other girl in the middle of the lake on a raft and take off for a little bit." She had told Maurice about the incident. "I mean, I can go swimmin' but I have a fear of being under the water for any period of time."

And there was a second terrorizing experience. Amanda and a teenage friend had nearly drowned in a swollen creek. "So that was part of the reason why I couldn't get into the water and save that hat. I wanted to save it because I knew it meant a lot to him."

With the decision made to leave the hat and head home, Amanda offered to drive. Why? The detectives wanted to know. "I don't know," she said. "It was a gut feeling."

Was Maurice smoking or drinking? Massey asked. Amanda couldn't explain her concern beyond having "a sick feeling."

When Maurice insisted he would drive, Amanda told him she wanted to get the kids out of the car and wait for him to back out.

Why did you feel that was necessary? Massey asked.

It was just Maurice being Maurice, Amanda explained. There was no fight, no harsh words as they all took their seats in the car.

"So I told him, 'Put your foot on the brake and the gas so it don't go forward.' He just told me, 'Okay, I know.' But the more I remembered and everything, especially since I had been there before and with people, I don't think there's any way if it was in reverse..." Amanda's voice trailed off. She was trying to connect ideas police suggested with what she remembered.

Maurice said, "Hold on, you guys," as he turned to look over his shoulder and stepped on the gas, Amanda told the officers.

"I felt the tires spin," Amanda recalled. "I don't think that car was in reverse. And I think the reason why the tires spun is he had his foot on the brake and the gas."

The detectives didn't challenge Amanda's assumptions that, when examined closely, could support a claim that the car went into the lake accidentally, that if Maurice pulled down on the gear shift as he was looking over his shoulder, the car could have been yanked into drive, shooting it into the lake where he panicked and put it into reverse—but too late to change the course of what had happened.

Such assumptions didn't fit the police theory.

Hawn encouraged her to keep talking, to let the story flow.

With water rushing into the car, Amanda turned to free Kyleigh from her seat. She didn't see Maurice leave the car.

"I couldn't get the car seat undone. All I could think to do was call 911."

Amanda recalled escaping through the driver's door and surprising Maurice in the water. "He didn't expect to see me come out of there."

"Why?" asked Hawn.

"He wanted us all gone."

The investigators glanced at one another, trying not to betray the importance of the threshold Amanda had just crossed, finally providing a statement that incriminated her boyfriend. This was just the kind of breakthrough they were hoping for—a first step towards the murder charges they were convinced the two would be facing.

Hawn suggested only a strong forward motion of the car would bring a rush of water into the vehicle with a sudden splash on the windshield. "You said you don't think he put it in reverse. Did he put it in drive and gun it?"

Amanda only knew that the car went into the water with such force that it caused everyone to panic.

Massey still had important dots to connect. Why did Amanda now believe Maurice wanted to kill the family?

Amanda offered an a la carte list for detectives to choose from: "Because of all the things that have happened with our relationship and him knowing that I had a fear of the water. And knowing that the kids weren't good at swimming. Because our relationship was with high turmoil and stress."

"Do you think he chose this time to do harm to you and the kids?" Massey inquired.

"Yes."

It was a notion police had not heard before and were unprepared to process.

"What makes you think that?" Massey asked, pursuing motive. Why would Maurice want to kill the woman who provided much of what he currently enjoyed?

Maurice has a selfish personality, Amanda said. And an intense hatred for her and the children.

For two weeks now, the drownings had brought penetrating scrutiny of her actions by police, and Amanda was assembling her own theory and beginning to look out for herself as the female investigator had urged her to do.

"I think he chose that moment because he was thinking that he could get away with it, that no one would find us and he would have enough time to get away."

Smoldering embers of an investigation were beginning to throw off some sparks. Yet with no evidence of direct threats by Maurice against Amanda or her children, and no distinct motive, Amanda's new story left police with a long way to go.

Chapter Eleven

So Amanda's story had been altered, now implicating Maurice in a deliberate act of killing her children. She had blended new details into her previous accounts of what had occurred that day, including damning allegations that Maurice was a gangbanger with access to guns. Detectives had uncovered nothing that confirmed those claims but they appreciated any negative implications that could be drawn towards Maurice. What was important at this moment, though, was why her story was changing.

"Because I want justice for my kids," she said. "I love them so much." Amanda seemed to still be trying to make sense of the tragedy.

"Why didn't you tell us this in the beginning?" Massey asked.

She was in shock, she said, walling off the terrible event as best she could.

Did conversations with other people help improve Amanda's memory?

"I've talked to God. I'm not a real religious person, but I've prayed every single day," she said.

The sheriff told Amanda her behavior with Maurice since the drownings sure didn't look like she feared him. She had broken ties with her family and stayed with him until just hours earlier when her friend picked her up.

Things had changed in recent days, she said. She didn't even want to be around him.

Massey explored the source of Amanda's fear. Had Maurice admitted to her that he intended to kill her and her children? No, Amanda said. It was just because of everything that had happened, not something he had said since the drownings.

And what about Maurice's statement about the need to get their stories straight?

"I have no idea. I didn't even know that he said that. I tried talking to him about it on the phone," Amanda told the sheriff. "I asked him why he didn't help me get my babies out of the car. And he wouldn't say nothin'."

Massey didn't buy the idea Amanda and Maurice in recent days had never talked through what happened at the lake.

"I talk about my kids," she answered. "He says that he misses them, too, but he can't think about anything because of the investigators and people looking at him and staring at him and that he don't even want to talk about it because he don't want to re-live it."

Hawn and Massey took Amanda moment-by-moment through how the car went into the lake. When her recollections didn't match the investigators' theory, they suggested her memory was faulty.

It was now nearly 10 a.m. and Amanda had let the county prosecutor's office know she would not be at her 9 a.m. traffic court hearing. As the questioning moved into its fifth hour, Massey told Amanda the goal was to find truth—not place blame. "You're not in trouble here," he said. "You just need to tell us what happened."

But Hawn implied things could go in another direction. "There is ample information and evidence—the statements from you and Maurice and experts, and the tests that were done—for us to move forward with this if that's what we need to do. The only thing that can benefit you is the truth."

"I want to tell the truth. I just can't remember," said Amanda, growing more upset.

The ease with which Amanda changed details of her story concerned the investigators. They needed a solid version to support the most serious charges of murder, but her inability to explain some of her claims against Maurice could lead investigators to a dead end.

Massey had reserved one card from his deck of personal life experiences, one that might help generate a common bond with Amanda. He, too, had lost a child. His 17-year-old daughter had died in a car crash five years earlier.

"I know your pain, Amanda. You know I've been through that," said the sheriff. The truth, he said, would help her keep her children alive in her memory. "I do that every day."

Amanda looked at Massey. She remembered the accident.

Hawn offered some rationale for why Amanda didn't—couldn't—have all the details exactly correct at the beginning. Maurice had coached her after police began asking questions, painting a revised picture of what had happened, as he pinned her against the dumpster, even as the car sank deeper into the water, her children desperate for help.

"As we progress through all this, Maurice got scared. He was afraid he was gonna get in trouble and he started coaching you," Hawn said, writing his own script of what took place.

"He's never said anything about what to say to you guys," Amanda responded. "He told me not to talk to you guys and I went against him and came here and talked to you."

When Amanda seemed unclear as to what Hawn meant by "coaching," he suggested maybe Maurice just told Amanda his version of what had happened, hoping she would adopt it as her own and repeat it to police.

But Amanda was unwilling to change her story to further implicate Maurice. It was time for Massey to play his pre-determined trump card.

"I'm sure you didn't notice it but there's a pole at that boat ramp. There's a camera on it," he said. "It recorded everything that happened. They had some problems with the video," he added as matter-of-factly as he could. "But we will have the video to show what was going on at the ramp."

He carefully observed Amanda's reaction.

"Good," she said. "Then when you get the videotape fixed, you can even see that he grabbed me. He said I was not goin' back in the water." Amanda seemed pleased and convinced video would confirm her story.

Now the investigators were frustrated, even desperate. In fact, there was no camera, no video—only a futile hope the ruse would unnerve Amanda. It had not.

State investigator Halloran stepped into the interview room. He had been watching through the glass. It was time to pile on. Tall, with a jawed sternness that intimidated many a suspect, Halloran reiterated how this moment was Amanda's final chance to deliver the truth.

"We want to help you through this. But the hammer is gonna fall," he warned. "It's gonna fall on you. It's gonna fall on Maurice." There was one thing Amanda could do to keep the hammer from crushing her: Firmly place the blame on Maurice.

"If we were to know that you tried to stop this from happening and save your kids, and Maurice didn't allow you to do that, if you had taken some steps--you wanted to go in the water and you were not allowed to because Maurice stopped you—that changes the whole equation."

Halloran was in Amanda's face. "You'll never be able to live with yourself unless this all comes out today." Then he heaped on the emotional trauma, giving voice to a reliving of the horrible final moments of the children's lives.

"They're not lookin' for Maurice." Halloran's every word was like an arrow aimed to penetrate Amanda's deepest sense of guilt. "They're lookin' for mommy. And they need mommy to help them at this point. Mommy, save me! Mommy, help, help! I can't get out, Mommy! Mommy!" Halloran was nearly shouting, imagining what had taken place inside the car. Amanda wouldn't abandon her children in a sinking car, he submitted. Someone must have prevented her from attempting a rescue. "And that person was Maurice, right?"

Austin Brown, age 3, Kyleigh Hamm, 23 months, and their brother, Christopher Hamm, age 6. (Family photo via Calvert Funeral Home)

Amanda Hamm in Clinton
High School 1995 yearbook.

Amanda Hamm booking photo
taken at DeWitt County, Ill.,
jail, December 2003.

Maurice LaGrone Jr. booking photo,
DeWitt County jail, December, 2003.

The boat ramp at Clinton Lake where Maurice LaGrone Jr. parked on Sept. 2, 2003. (*The Pantagrah*/David Proeber)

An Illinois Department of Conservation officer collected toys and stuffed animals from the area where the car went into Clinton Lake. (*The Pantagraph*/Steve Smedley)

Family and friends offered support to Amanda Hamm as her three children were laid to rest at Memorial Park Cemetery in Clinton, Ill. (*The Pantagraph*/David Proeber)

Ann Powers held photos of her three dead grandchildren during a media interview in December 2003. (*The Pantagraph*/Steve Smedley)

Maurice LaGrone Jr. in a photo provided to the media by
his lawyers before the start of his trial in early 2006.

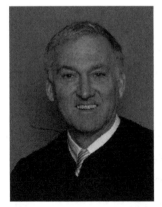

Jeff Justice, defense lawyer
for Maurice LaGrone Jr.

Thomas Griffith, defense lawyer
for Maurice LaGrone Jr. (Photo/
Decatur Bar Association)

Special prosecutor Ed Parkinson receives a hug from Susan Baldis, Kyleigh Hamm's grandmother, following the 2006 trial of Maurice LaGrone Jr. (*The Pantagraph*/David Proeber)

Special prosecutor Roger Simpson (left) and DeWitt County Sheriff Roger Massey talk to the media following the LaGrone trial. (The Pantagraph/David Proeber)

Amanda Hamm is escorted to the courtroom for her 2006 trial on murder charges. (*Herald & Review*/Lyndsie Schlink)

Steve Skelton, Amanda Hamm's lawyer, answers reporters' questions after her trial. (*Herald & Review*/Kelly J. Huff)

Amanda Hamm (center) is escorted from the Dwight
Correctional Center by her mother Ann Powers and stepfather
Lindy Powers. (*The Pantagraph*/David Proeber)

Gravesites of the three siblings were decorated at Memorial
Park Cemetery. (*The Pantagraph*/David Proeber)

"Yes," Amanda responded, struggling to keep up with Halloran's running version of what took place.

Halloran pushed forward, slowing down only briefly to insert an occasional question into the narrative. He was setting her up to confirm a crucial part of his theory.

How long did Maurice hold her back from water as the car sank?

There was a pause. Then Amanda cautiously estimated Maurice restrained her for four or five minutes as the car slid farther into the lake, the children inside. Only then did he allow her to make the call to 911, Amanda told the officers.

This was new information, important information, Halloran said. He altered his approach.

"Did you know that after you die, they can check your blood and determine how long you've been dead? So we can match up your story with the blood work and see if those children were taken out of the water immediately after they drowned, or whether there was a delay."

Halloran watched to see if Amanda understood what he was saying. He couldn't tell. She looked exhausted.

"Here's why I asked you that question. I already knew the answer to it. I wanted to see if you were gonna tell me."

But like the phantom surveillance camera, definitive proof of how long the children had been in the lake did not exist. That determination would prove difficult for authorities to pin down.

With Maurice targeted as the perpetrator of a crime, Halloran sought to add more bricks to the walls that were closing around the suspect. "Now this is something very important," he told Amanda. When did Maurice first suggest that life would be easier without the children?

"He never has. He's never said nothing like that to me," said Amanda.

The investigators looked at each other, trying to sense whether there was a consensus on how to proceed.

Halloran became less confrontational. Amanda's accusations about Maurice, he said, could be confirmed through a lie detector test, something he considered "very accurate," something police may ask her to do.

What had now been more than six hours of interrogation was taking its toll on Amanda as investigators asked her to walk them through the sequence of events one last time. She responded to the same questions she had heard and responded to so many times before, but now she paused each time.

"Amanda, the truth is easy," Halloran prodded. "You should be able to tell me the truth without having to think about it. The fact that you're hesitating now tells me that you are starting to think of another story to tell me and I don't want to hear it."

Amanda sat silent for several minutes. Halloran continued to nudge her to repeat the details of what had led to the deaths of her children. Then he pushed her.

"You've got to do this for your kids, Amanda. This is their only chance at ever getting any peace—what you know now, when you've played this through your mind. This was no accident, was it?"

"No," said Amanda.

Halloran's experience told him he was nearing a breakthrough, a complete confession. "Walk me through it, Amanda."

"I don't even understand it myself."

Like a confessor trying to exorcise a demon from a penitent, Halloran did everything but reach inside Amanda and physically pull the words from her body.

"The truth is so much easier than a story. It's inside you. Unlock it. Get it out now."

"I want to go home." Fresh out of any new details to add to her version, Amanda was nearly worn down to her last breath. The detectives ignored her request.

"How do you think you would do in a lie detector test right now, huh?" Halloran asked. "You want me to hook you up to that machine and use these same questions? How do you think you're gonna do?"

"I don't know," Amanda said, withdrawing into her chair and silence as Halloran laid out the threat to force her to submit to a polygraph.

We need to know what happened between the time the car went into the water and when the boater arrived, Halloran insisted. "The kids are alive—the kids are dead. We need to put what happened in the middle and you need to get it straight."

Cooperation could have its benefits for a single mother living under a load of stress, Halloran suggested. He described how it could work.

"Do you think maybe this person could get through with maybe some counseling, some therapy, that they could get their life back on track? That this person is somebody we should take a look at giving a second chance to?"

"Yes," Amanda agreed.

"And the person responsible for deliberately drowning three children, should he get a second chance or face serious consequences?"

"Go to prison for the rest of his life," she said.

And what should happen to you, Amanda?"

"Be out here," she said, separating her culpability from her boyfriend's.

Reluctant to let Amanda leave without securing what he needed, Halloran ignored Amanda on her second, third and fourth requests to go home.

"Let's take a break for a cigarette. Then we'll talk some more."

By the time the smoke break ended, so had the day's long interrogation. But investigators wouldn't give up their effort to get Amanda to volunteer key information they required. Tomorrow was another day.

Chapter Twelve

Amanda's fears that Maurice had wanted her and the children dead led Massey to offer her a motel room in Forsyth, 20 miles south of Clinton, as a safe haven for the night. Peavler, still in her dual role as a police source and Amanda's confidante, offered to stay with her.

The motel stay gave Amanda a break for the night from the long grueling day of questioning. It also kept her within Massey's line of sight until her planned return for more conversation the next day.

Once Amanda and Peavler were inside their room at the Comfort Inn, Amanda took a shower and ordered a pizza for delivery to the motel. She talked briefly with Peavler about the children, remembering the fun things they used to do. When the conversation turned to Sept. 2, Peavler asked Amanda why they had gone to the lake. It was a place to go that was free, Amanda told her.

As the two talked, it was clear Amanda couldn't let go of Maurice's greatest wrong, his fondness for other women. His lack of loyalty to her, combined with the physical abuse she had suffered at his hands, could put Maurice in a bad light with police, creating new legal headaches for him, Amanda told Peavler. And that was okay. A few sobering problems would serve him right, kind of an atonement for his failure as a boyfriend.

Conscious of the heavy media attention on the drowning deaths, Peavler suggested Amanda stay behind in the room after dinner while Peavler went to a nearby mall to buy herself clothes for the next day. Amanda slept, briefly waking when Peavler returned, to tell her that Peavler's boyfriend, Craig Brown, had called. Amanda continued to sleep as Peavler watched TV. She woke again at about 7 p.m., watched TV with Peavler and then walked with her to a nearby gas station to buy cigarettes.

They turned out the lights shortly after midnight.

A call from Brown woke the two women just before 8 a.m.—later than Peavler had intended to sleep. Over the motel's complimentary breakfast, Amanda spoke to Peavler in hushed tones about fresh recollections that had visited her as she tried to fall asleep. Among them: Amanda now remembered escaping the car through the passenger side window rather than the driver's side.

Before leaving the table, Amanda used her cell phone in an unsuccessful attempt to reach her grandmother. Peavler surmised Amanda wanted to ask her grandmother about relatives in the Chicago area who might be willing to put her up for a while.

On their drive north to the sheriff's department, Amanda repeated a comment she said Maurice made as they were sitting on the boat ramp: "Wouldn't it be fucked up if the car went into the water?" And she remembered suggesting to Maurice, after they had both escaped the car, that they try to break a window to rescue the children. He rejected the idea, saying shattering glass could harm the kids.

After just a few minutes of talking during the drive to Clinton, Amanda shut down the conversation. She turned on the radio, rather pointedly letting Peavler know additional disclosures would be saved for police.

When they reached the sheriff's department, the two women met with different teams of investigators. Peavler brought two Illinois State police agents up-to-date on what Amanda had been doing and saying. Down the hall, Halloran and Massey were prepared for their sixth session with Amanda, again with no attorney present.

The sheriff began. Did either of the adults in the car intend to hurt the children?

"No, I did not intend to. He never came out and said that he intended to," said Amanda.

When the car started to move forward into the lake, Amanda said she told Maurice "stop the fuckin' car." "I told him to just throw it in park or something. And the car had already hit the water by that time."

As the level of water rose in the vehicle, she said, so did the panic.

"Next thing I knew he was looking for the lock to unlock the door because when you put the car into gear, it automatically locks. He got the door unlocked, opened the door and got out."

Amanda felt terror as she tried to grab the children from the back seat. Water splashed against her chest.

"God, I hate myself. I panicked and got out of the car from my side through the window."

Now, she was saying, Maurice held her back from the car as it dipped hood-first into the lake. And after she made the 911 call and they went back down the hill towards the water, he continued to restrain her, even from rushing to her babies after they had been pulled from the water.

Massey steered Amanda back to her thoughts about Maurice, about his rough-housing with her kids, how it may have indicated his intention to harm them—all useful information for investigators trying to build their case.

The children drove Maurice nuts, she said. "He'd get irritated because they wanted me all the time."

The move to St. Louis planned for the following spring, however, may have meant a break from Christopher and Austin if Amanda's mother could keep them for what was left of the school year. Maurice liked the idea of having only one child around, she said.

Halloran asked Amanda to explain why she was again willing to talk to police without an attorney.

"I had so many nightmares and things that I couldn't remember and they started comin' back to me. And I knew I needed to get it out for my kids. I love 'em so much."

She was crying.

"Amanda, is what you've told us today the truth?" Halloran asked.

"Yes, it is," she assured him.

"Okay, if that's the truth, we're gonna need to clean you up a bit. You understand what I mean by that? Because you've got some statements you said before, okay?"

Worried that investigators were suggesting she was lying, Amanda tried to explain why details of her stories seemed to change with each interview. Remembering was difficult, she said.

"Everything was so confusing and dark and buried so deep inside of me and it started to come out. I can't really explain it. It's like the kids are with me, helpin' me through this."

On the question of how she left the flooding car, Amanda claimed she had lowered the window a bit to allow smoke from a last-minute cigarette to escape. Then a push of the electronic button sent the window down the rest of the way, allowing her to make her exit.

There was more to clear up. What did Amanda mean when she told Maurice at the hospital to "stay strong?" And why at the hospital did she tell her close friend, Bev Clymer, that Maurice's foot had slipped off the brake?

Amanda said she couldn't remember making either statement, that maybe her friend had misunderstood.

Halloran wanted Amanda to get inside her lover's head. What about his comment that things would be "fucked up" if the car went into the lake? What did that mean?

"That he wanted us all dead. And when I came out of the car, he looked totally surprised to see me and was just standin' there."

An essential piece of Amanda's analysis still puzzled Massey. Why would Maurice want her dead?

"Because I would never let up on the cheating and I wanted the truth. And because I was constantly tellin' him to get out. Then I'd take him back. And because he didn't like the fact that I let the kids be on me like they were."

Amanda's explanation allowed her to punish Maurice for his sins against her but it didn't mesh with what police knew about her boyfriend's history with women. When he grew tired of girlfriends, his pattern was to just pack up and move on; he didn't kill them. Other times, women asked him—and he agreed—to leave when they became weary of his inability to hold a steady job.

After about 45 minutes of questioning, Amanda asked for a short break. When the interview resumed, the investigators told her they were ready to end the meeting. It was, they said, her last chance to add anything to what she had already told them—30 seconds, they said, to provide more details.

"The next person we're talking to is Maurice," Halloran warned. "So if you need to tell us something, you've got to do it now."

Amanda left police with a document: a 95-word statement that provided her view of Maurice's actions.

"From going through details and memories from the night everything happened I remember as the car went into the water screaming at Maurice to stop the car or through (*sic*) it into park or something. I turned back around to get Kyleigh and he put his hands up to the gear shift. I thought he was going to put it in park and he told me he couldn't, and he reached for the door and got out of the car. I was yelling at him to help me and he didn't he continued to get out."

Amanda's written words still failed to produce a consistent calculation of what Maurice may have been thinking and what he was doing as the car rolled into the water. Even her new recollections were a blend of fears and incriminating thoughts about Maurice that bowed to her repeated assertions that he had no specific plan to kill anyone.

Police set aside denials that didn't fit their theory that the man behind the wheel was an abuser capable of acting on a hated for Amanda and her children.

Her effort to blend her boyfriend's violent tendencies and her incompetence had kept her out of police custody. But she couldn't escape the grief and guilt she bore every waking moment.

Chapter Thirteen

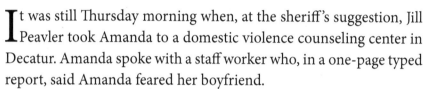

It was still Thursday morning when, at the sheriff's suggestion, Jill Peavler took Amanda to a domestic violence counseling center in Decatur. Amanda spoke with a staff worker who, in a one-page typed report, said Amanda feared her boyfriend.

The worker drove to Clinton to retrieve some things Amanda had left at the sheriff's office. There, Massey told the counselor Amanda's family and friends didn't want her around them and he didn't blame them. There were no restrictions on Amanda, he said, but she might be suicidal.

Amanda was moved to Dove, a Decatur domestic abuse shelter. As she arrived, Amanda pleaded "I want my mom," saying "she won't talk to me…because I didn't get out of a bad relationship soon enough."

Shelter staff members took notes as Amanda recounted her history as a victim of sexual abuse, substance abuse that occurred in her late teens and physical abuse at the hands of Maurice. He would beat and choke her, she said, and threaten to kill her or her family. She had kicked him out of their apartment several times but always let him return. "I'd get scared and he'd promise to change and help me," she said.

She also recounted Maurice's remarks as she left for police interviews several days earlier. "We'll have a nice fucking talk when you return," were his words, Amanda said, continuing her effort to place blame on her boyfriend.

The next night Amanda told a Dove staffer she was going to hang herself, a threat that led to her being taken to a local hospital with a psychiatric unit.

St. Mary's Hospital overlooks Lake Decatur in the southern end of the blue-collar community with a history of chronic economic struggles. Factories once its life blood had closed their doors or sent workers home, temporary layoff slips in hand. With one of the few psychiatric units in central Illinois, the hospital was a revolving door for people who lacked financial resources to stay there long enough to fully recover.

"I have no reason to live anymore," Amanda told nurses in St. Mary's emergency room. She had already tried to hang herself, she said, and if given the chance, she would try again.

Amanda's prior suicide attempts at ages 14 and 17 were documented by staff. When asked if she had children, Amanda said, "yes and no" and began to cry.

An emergency room doctor obtained more information from Amanda. The children were dead, she said, and it was possible her boyfriend wanted them to die. A nurse noted Amanda was grieving and crying but no tears were visible. The intent to commit suicide was serious enough that the doctor admitted Amanda to the seventh-floor psychiatric unit.

The next day, a hospital chaplain talked with Amanda. The loss of contact with family and friends angry over the deaths of the children left Amanda feeling cut off from the world. But she had a hard time talking with mental health professionals about those feelings, she volunteered. Feelings were kept buried beneath layers of trauma that brought her to the brink of self-destruction. Her mental state didn't improve over the next 24 hours. She cried, saying she didn't want to live without her children.

Sheriff Massey called the psychiatric unit, wanting to schedule still another interview with Amanda. She had included him on her contact list at the hospital—still intent on cooperating with police. But now Amanda told members of the nursing staff she really didn't want to see him.

After wavering back and forth on whether it was a good idea, Amanda talked to her mother, who in turn sought advice from her former boss, retired DeWitt County state's attorney Richard Koritz. He suggested Amanda answer Massey's questions. Cooperation would be viewed more favorably than resistance, he counseled. The visit was scheduled for Monday, Sept. 22—the day Kyleigh would have turned two.

With no one counseling her otherwise, Amanda agreed to meet with police and take a polygraph exam. Based on investigators' earlier suggestion that a lie detector test would confirm her truthfulness, she believed it was in her best interest to cooperate.

That morning Massey, Hawn and several state police agents met at the sheriff's department to plan the hospital visit, pleased Amanda's doctor had approved it.

With the investigators was Mark Murphy, a state police polygraph examiner. Together, they consulted with special prosecutor Simpson. He reminded them to record all portions of their meeting with Amanda, not specifying whether the recording should be audio, video—or both. Meanwhile Murphy discussed with Halloran the questions he would use in a polygraph exam, even though the final call was up to Murphy. He ultimately decided to focus on whether the drownings were premeditated.

Investigators knew a jury would never be told of the results—or even the existence--of the polygraph exam because such evidence was inadmissible, but they viewed it as a tool that might persuade Amanda to reconsider her answers to their most incriminating questions.

It was decided Massey, Halloran and Panizo, along with Murphy, would constitute the team that would make the trip to Decatur that afternoon.

They pulled into St. Mary's parking lot around 2 p.m., determined to nail down inconsistencies in Amanda's account of the children's deaths. Although it would be a future topic of dispute, the officers would later insist they took no recording device into the secured hospital ward.

Amanda was taking three psychotropic medications to help with sleep, stabilize her mood and overcome depression. Her day leading up to the meeting was the same as others: She remained depressed, anxious and tearful. She told hospital staffers she didn't feel comfortable moving from her secured room to the psychiatric ward's open unit where she'd have contact with other patients.

Before he started, Murphy reviewed Amanda's medications, consulting a reference stored on his computer for information about how they could affect polygraph results. He was satisfied there was no issue.

When Amanda was escorted to the room by a hospital staffer, the polygraph technician was surprised by her appearance. She looked less haggard and frightened than she had appeared in her mugshot. But she had lost a noticeable amount of weight, despite the hospital's efforts to keep pounds on by giving Amanda ice cream and supplement drinks.

Murphy began by asking Amanda a series of background questions, a kind of warm-up and baseline. According to a written report (the only record that exists), Amanda told Murphy she had tried to kill herself because she wanted to be with her children in heaven.

The actual polygraph exam lasted about an hour. Amanda answered Murphy's questions as Halloran sat just five feet away.

The written report of the interview and polygraph says Amanda's version of events was substantially similar to her other interviews.

But deception, the report said, was noted on responses to five questions in which she denied the most damning accusations:

*Did she plan or arrange with Maurice to drive the car into the lake?

*Did she and Maurice ever talk about getting rid of the kids?

*Did Maurice ever say anything in her presence about hurting the children?

*After the car went into the lake and Amanda got out of the water, did Maurice prevent her from going back to the car?

*And was she withholding any information from the police about what occurred?

Halloran asked Murphy to remain in the room for the next phase of the interrogation. The good rapport Murphy had developed with Amanda during the pre-test interview might be helpful in ongoing questioning.

Amanda had juice brought to her by the hospital staff, then agreed to continue with post-polygraph questions. She signed another acknowledgement of her Miranda rights.

Together Halloran and Murphy revealed the polygraph results to Amanda and asked her to explain the discrepancies.

Halloran employed the same practice he had used in other interviews to get Amanda to provide new information. She had a limited time—10 minutes, he said—to produce the truth or he and Murphy would leave.

Murphy added his own threat. "I've got better things to do than this shit. My wife is in the hospital," he said. "I'm leaving." But he didn't.

Emotionally and physically drained, Amanda agreed to continue. Her statements, some of them enclosed in quotation marks, were recorded in a written report Halloran authored the next day. In a dozen instances, Amanda's response is rendered as an affirmative nod, starting with a pledge to tell the truth.

Along the lengthy interview, there was discussion about the need to make an audio or video recording. Murphy would later tell defense lawyers that someone in the group said basically "Screw it" when it came time to decide if the process should be delayed while a recorder was retrieved from a vehicle. Murphy said Halloran didn't disagree. There was no certainty they'd even be allowed to bring a recorder into the psychiatric unit.

But Amanda would later recall a tape recorder being present, having been brought into the room by one of the detectives who asked her to wait to answer his question while he set up something behind her.

Regardless, an audio recording would not have chronicled Amanda's nods that came to be viewed as admissions to the most incriminating statements yet: Yes, she knew Maurice planned to harm the children, a plan that involved putting the car in the lake with the children inside.

But she was still unable, or unwilling, to deliver any specific details of discussions the couple may have had about killing the children. She referred once again to her boyfriend's menacing conduct with Christopher and Austin.

Surely, Halloran insisted, there must have been some planning that preceded the trip to the lake.

"Nothing was discussed until we were on our way to the boat ramp," Amanda said. "As soon as we got out there and started going around the curve, I knew the kids were in danger."

She continued her story, adding new details. Notes from the interview indicate Maurice said something about his plan of driving fast and plunging off the dock, then later mentioned the car going off the boat ramp.

"I knew Maurice was planning an accident and something was going to happen—but I didn't know what kind," the report says Amanda told the officers.

There was a knock on the door. It was Sheriff Massey, wanting to confer with Halloran and Murphy outside the interview room. The hospital staff, he told them, wanted the interview wrapped up. Amanda had been with them for seven hours now.

A hospital staff member escorted Amanda from the room.

Police left the hospital with fresh allegations Maurice had planned to sink the car in the lake with his girlfriend and her children inside. But the facts did not neatly bind the two adults together in the murderous maneuver theorized by police.

They turned their attention back to Maurice. His reaction to his girlfriend's accusations could bring the investigation home, they thought, if they were able to get him to confirm enough of what Amanda had just said.

Three days later, Massey and Panizo met with Maurice in an interview room at the Bloomington Police Department. He signed a consent to have the interview audio and video recorded. They asked Maurice to submit to a polygraph. He refused.

The sheriff briefed Maurice on recent developments in the investigation, starting with a statement about a record that existed of the recent interview with Amanda.

"We have got a complete taped statement from her," he said. "Basically, her defense here is a battered woman defense. She's been in a shelter. She's now in a psychiatric ward."

For his own good, the sheriff counseled, Maurice needed to respond to his girlfriend's damning accusations that he controlled and abused her to the point that she would do anything for him. "I think it's gonna be important here for you to get on the record and counter that in some way, shape or form," Massey said. "She's put it all on you."

After most of an hour, Maurice had not wavered from his contention that it was all a tragic accident. The sheriff had done most of the talking.

Sure, Massey said, if Maurice was willing to take the blame and carry the whole load for what happened to the children, that was his choice. There were some in the community who would be happy with that scenario.

"People cheering right behind you because you're a black man. You got your white woman. You got three white kids. There will be some people right behind this thing and thinkin' it's all you.

"I've grown up with Amanda in that town," Massey continued. "So I know her past drug use. I know she went out and tried to trap every man she's ever had and she's tried to get pregnant to keep them so she could have a husband."

Amanda would not avoid criminal consequences for her role in the deaths, the sheriff told Maurice. But Maurice, the sheriff said, could face nine counts of homicide and the death penalty.

Maurice stood his ground and shut off discussion. He would place his faith in God, he said.

What turned out to be the last opportunity police would have with Maurice ended when he asked to speak with his father. Massey said Maurice Sr. was involved in his own interview with police. However, no reports were ever produced that document an interview with Maurice's father.

Without a solid confession from Maurice or Amanda, police would turn their focus to others who knew the couple. They would have to build their murder case on who Maurice and Amanda are, rather than what they may have done.

Chapter Fourteen

Law enforcement was in Roger Massey's blood. His father, Don, had been the county's sheriff from 1978 to 1986. The younger Massey joined the department as a dispatcher when he was just 16, moving up the ranks under his father.

As sheriff, he oversaw patrols and crime prevention in the 405 square miles that included Clinton and a half dozen villages. He also supervised a 90-bed county jail. Though it typically housed no more than a couple dozen locals—usually low-level hoods awaiting trial— the jail was often filled with criminals from elsewhere. In fact, the DeWitt County government relied on a $400,000 annual contract with the U.S. Bureau of Prisons to make ends meet.

Roger Massey was proud of his jail. But he had found himself in the unwelcome glare of national media attention in February of 2001 when one of his federal prisoners escaped.

Clayton Lee Waagner was on the FBI's "Most Wanted" list after his escape through a vent he discovered in a closet adjacent to his DeWitt County cell. Waagner was a convicted bank robber and anti-abortion activist awaiting sentencing on firearms and auto theft convictions. While on the loose and only a couple months after the Sept. 11 terrorist attacks on America, he sent 280 letters that claimed to contain anthrax to Planned Parenthood offices. After a 10-month manhunt, Waagner was captured in Ohio and never returned to DeWitt County.

The Waagner case had taught Massey an important lesson in how to deal with the media: Tight control of information was everything, and the public's perception of how law enforcement was doing its job could be as important as actual results.

Now the media was seeking updates on the drowning investigation. Massey had been doing regular press briefings but then stopped them. They had become a distraction and he had little new he was willing to share. Even so, a stack of phone messages from reporters awaited him each time he returned to his desk.

Amanda had been in the psychiatric unit 18 nights when she was released Oct. 7 and returned to the domestic violence shelter. Before she left the hospital, she spoke with Maurice on the phone. Sheriff Massey talked with her at the shelter, but only long enough to learn she'd be making no further statements without the advice of an attorney.

Amanda asked Jill Peavler to pick her up at the shelter and take her to Bloomington where she knew more people. Peavler made the 50-mile trip to Decatur and took Amanda by Maurice's home. His stepmother said he had gone to St. Louis to talk with an attorney.

After she dropped off Amanda at a Bloomington women's shelter, Peavler called Detective Hawn and reported details of her contact with Amanda. She called again several days later to say Amanda was working at a Steak 'n Shake restaurant in Bloomington.

Maurice returned from St. Louis and informed Amanda their relationship was over. Amanda brushed off the news; a restaurant co-worker had caught her eye.

But the split with her family still left Amanda without the emotional support she craved as she grieved over the loss of her children. In a lengthy, rambling voice mail she left for her mother Oct. 18, Amanda lashed out:

"I just called to let you know that I love you and this is the last time that I am going to talk to you....I did love my kids and I fucked up that night and I will never live it down in myself and I've always been the black sheep in this family and I'm sorry I let your grandkids down and I will never ever ever ever forgive myself. And another thing. You were never ever there for me either and I've come to realize that, along with everything, you are not sticking by me and I understand why and I don't fault you for that but I can have no contact with you. I can't deal with you guys not loving me, because you don't. If you did, you would be there for me."

She went on to wish a good and happy life for her mother and Lindy Powers. She would pray for them every night, she said, and hope for forgiveness from them and from God "for everything that I've ever done wrong in my life."

Lindy Powers called police. Massey went to the Powers home and made a copy of Amanda's message to her family.

Let go from her new restaurant job and without a love interest, Amanda connected once again with Maurice. It was the same day she had left the voice mail for her family. The two were together on Saturday and went to church and dinner with his family on Sunday. The outing helped Amanda deal with how she had been snubbed by family and friends, even as they organized a fundraiser to help pay expenses.

In early November, Amanda was ready to get legal help and face down the threats from police. During a walk in downtown Bloomington, some six blocks from the homeless shelter where she was staying, she spotted the law office of Steven Skelton. She stopped at the busy intersection near the county jail and made a mental note of his name. When she called his office later, he agreed to meet with her.

Skelton was one of the area's best-known criminal defense attorneys, having been involved in several death penalty cases. In fact, when Amanda arranged to meet him at his small office, Skelton was representing an already-convicted serial killer, Andrew Urdiales, in a murder case in neighboring Livingston County.

Skelton had seen media coverage about what had happened at Clinton Lake. As Amanda gave her account of that day, Skelton assessed Amanda as being confused, lost and overwhelmed. He knew, from experience, she would automatically be a suspect in the children's deaths, a peril that had begun to dawn on Amanda as well.

After her sometimes halting description of the drowning incident, Skelton asked whether she had consulted with any other attorney.

Yes, she said. There was that brief discussion with Richard Goff, the former DeWitt County prosecutor whom she had briefly consulted with days after the drownings.

"I'm assuming you were told not to speak to the police and you've followed those instructions," Skelton said.

"No," Amanda answered.

Skelton looked up from the notes he was taking. "No, what? You weren't told you shouldn't talk with police?"

"No. I thought it would be okay. So I have. Lots of times."

Skelton felt like sliding under his desk. As Amanda described the number, length and flavor of the interrogations, Skelton's assessment of her situation grew more dire. The tearful young woman sitting in front of him, he concluded, was not only frightened and intimidated, but she had voluntarily given authorities information they could use to support any criminal theory they had come up with.

Amanda didn't seem surprised when Skelton told her that if she were charged with first degree murder, the death penalty was a possibility. As a member of the state's capital litigation bar, he said, he'd be eligible to represent her. If she couldn't afford an attorney, the court would appoint one. In that case, she couldn't select her own lawyer, but she could indicate her preference.

After an hour-long discussion, Amanda left Skelton's office feeling she found someone who could be on her side. He hadn't sugar-coated the serious legal trouble that loomed, but his honest assessment was as relieving as it was frightening; it's easier to confront a bad situation when you know its name and size.

In one of his increasingly rare public comments, Sheriff Massey cautioned the public not to read too much into a decision to dismiss Maurice's traffic ticket for driving under the influence of drugs. The charge could be reinstated at any time, Massey noted.

Other information was still weeks away, he said. "It's a complicated case. It's not that unusual for cases to go months and months and some over a year," he told a reporter.

The whereabouts of Maurice and Amanda were still being monitored by police. Maurice was unable to find work in Bloomington. Even a restaurant owner disposed toward giving felons a second chance wouldn't look him in the eye when Maurice stopped by to ask about a job. His connection to the drownings was too fresh and too firm. Maurice's family was relieved when he returned to St. Louis where he found work in a hotel and shared an apartment with a new girlfriend.

Meanwhile police still had Peavler's assistance in knowing what Amanda was doing, saying, maybe thinking.

On Nov. 5, Amanda was admitted to Chestnut Health Systems in Bloomington to receive mental health and substance abuse counseling. During her 23 days at the residential facility, she wrote several poems directed to God, her children and Maurice.

A poem, titled "Up in Heaven," dedicated to "my beautiful angels," reads in part:

> "I know you're in a better place now
> In heaven with God smiling down
> But I'm selfish I want you here with me
> Back to the way things used to be."

Another poem, authored the next day, amounts to an apology to Maurice for the damaging statements she made to police about him, statements she apparently regretted.

Titled "Repercussions of My Own Doing," the poem begins:
"I'm sorry
I know I was wrong
The spiteful things I did that were so hurtful to you
Something I don't know if I'll ever change or undo."

Amanda professed her love for Maurice, calling him the only man she had truly loved and tried to explain why she had laid the blame for the children's deaths on him:

"My only answer is:
Yes my love was strong
But my hate for myself and what was going on around me
        was stronger
So, I had to bring you down to the same 'hell' I was in
        and worse
And who better to do it to than you."

In a Nov. 18 entry saved on a Chestnut computer and later retrieved by police armed with a search warrant, Amanda wrote an open letter to God.

"Dear God-
Hello God it's me, Amanda
I have some questions to ask you.
My life has taken many twists and turns
I don't understand why
Why'd you do this to me?
All my life I wanted a big family
And at one point I had that family
It was my three children and me

For six, three and one year it was Me, Christopher, Austin
and Kyleigh
I didn't do anything wrong for this to happen to me.
Why my babies?"

After Amanda left the Chestnut treatment program Nov.
28, she landed at Home Sweet Home Mission, a homeless shelter
in Bloomington.

On Tuesday, Dec. 9—more than three months after the drownings—Maurice and Amanda were arrested by police in a coordinated maneuver.

At 3:20 p.m., Maurice was taken into custody as he headed to
his job at a St. Louis hotel. Amanda was arrested two hours later at
the homeless shelter in Bloomington. Yes, she was told, Maurice was
now in custody, too. She asked about the charges each would face.

Her body shuddered when she heard the answer: nine counts of
first-degree murder.

Chapter Fifteen

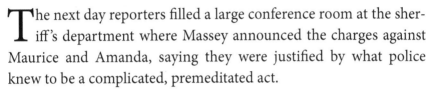

The next day reporters filled a large conference room at the sheriff's department where Massey announced the charges against Maurice and Amanda, saying they were justified by what police knew to be a complicated, premeditated act.

"You would have to be here two or three days to see the whole thing and understand it," said the sheriff, flanked by the six investigators who worked the case with him. Missing from the line-up was the special prosecutor. Roger Simpson would steer clear of the media throughout the legal proceedings.

Massey repeated for the national news audience the similarities he saw with the Susan Smith case. The goal of the investigation, he said, "is to try to disprove that this was an accident."

He wouldn't discuss possible motives, except to rule out a life insurance payout.

Keeping specifics under wraps was more important than ever, the sheriff told reporters eager to know what police had uncovered in three months of work.

If they're convicted, Massey explained, the murder suspects could face the death penalty.

The nine murder counts—three for each child—reflected different elements of the charges, including an accusation that Maurice intended to kill them while he was in control of the vehicle when it went into the lake, and that he knew his actions created a strong probability of death or great bodily harm to the youngsters.

The charges against Amanda were identical to those lodged against Maurice under an accountability provision of Illinois law. "This deals with holding her responsible for playing a part or failing to act," Massey explained. Her level of responsibility in the deaths matched her boyfriend's, he said, adding that he was confident police had gathered sufficient evidence to win convictions.

"Cops: It's murder," blazed the next day's headline in *The Pantagraph*, a Bloomington newspaper.

All eyes were on Amanda when she was brought into a DeWitt County courtroom. Dressed in a blue jail uniform and shackled at her ankles, she sobbed as Judge Stephen Peters read each of the charges. She shook her head as he told her the possible consequences: a prison term ranging from 60 years to life in prison or a death sentence.

With Amanda was Steve Skelton. The defense attorney she had met a few weeks earlier had been appointed to represent her. The fortuitous assignment was made by Judge Peters who, knowing the two had already talked, chose Skelton from a list of lawyers qualified to handle death penalty cases in Illinois.

Among the many spectators in the courtroom were Amanda's mother, her Aunt Kathy Clifton and other relatives. They clung to each other as they brushed past reporters following the 15-minute hearing.

Maurice was escorted into the courtroom next. He also shook his head in disbelief as the judge recited the murder charges. When asked if he wanted a public defender appointed, Maurice said he would hire his own lawyer. "I'm not sure how long it will take," Maurice told the judge.

Peters set a hearing for Dec. 24 to review Maurice's efforts to retain counsel.

Bond in each case was set at $5 million, meaning Amanda and Maurice would each have to come up with $500,000 to be released while they awaited trial. A grand jury would meet the following week to hear evidence in the case and presumably return indictments, allowing the state to avoid a public preliminary hearing before a judge to determine if enough evidence existed to hold the pair.

Skelton expressed doubts about a trial for his client in DeWitt County.

"The massive amount of media coverage makes a fair and impartial trial in the current venue unlikely," he told reporters.

Residents of the public housing where Amanda and Maurice had lived became sought-after media interviews. Any hint of suspicion—a raised voice heard through paper thin apartment walls or a comment from a child on the playground—was spun into a premonition that something didn't add up to the drownings being an accident.

"Most of us knew from the beginning that there had to be some kind of foul play," one neighbor told a reporter. "We just didn't want to believe it."

The neighbor knew about Amanda's plans to move to St. Louis and how the boys might stay with their grandmother until the end of the school year. Amanda had shared her dream of a college education with others, including one of Amanda's co-workers at Grecian Gardens.

"She asked for a day off to go to the school and find out about financial assistance," the co-worker recalled.

The long-awaited decision by authorities to charge the mother and her boyfriend with murder gave politicians an opportunity to grab a few headlines. In a letter to Illinois Governor Rod Blagojevich, two area lawmakers called for repeal of a moratorium on the death penalty. The pause in executions had been put in place 10 months earlier by then-Governor George Ryan, who cleared the state's death row after more than a dozen wrongfully convicted people were released.

The new capital murder cases in DeWitt County would become ground zero in a continuing debate about the death penalty in Illinois.

Pro bono lawyers working with exoneration projects at law schools had proven time and again how defendants had been wrongfully convicted for a variety of reasons, ranging from prosecutorial misconduct to false confessions and the use of lying jailhouse informants. Death penalty opponents argued exoneration of even one death row inmate demonstrates the system is flawed and puts the innocent at risk. Proponents maintained some of those freed had been let go on legal technicalities, and that the ultimate penalty should be available for the most cruel and heinous crimes.

With Maurice and Amanda locked up in separate pods in the DeWitt County jail not far from Ann Danison's desk at the state's attorney's office, the media focus shifted to family members who might talk about the murder charges. Amanda's mother was ready to share the feelings she had bottled up for months.

In her first comments to the media since the arrest, Danison said prison would be a sufficient penalty if her daughter were convicted. She would not support the death penalty for Amanda.

She still loved Amanda, she said, though the barrier she had established between them when Amanda insisted on remaining with Maurice still existed. And she still found the intense pain and loss of Sept. 2 overwhelming.

"When I saw her in court, I hurt for her," she said. "I'm her mother, and I wish I could have given her a hug. But there is this barrier. She took my grandkids, and I can't ever get them back."

Flaws in details Amanda and Maurice had given her about what happened at the lake started to surface after the funeral, she said. "All she would tell me was that she panicked. That was her only answer."

That stiffened the estrangement. "I didn't disown her. She's my daughter, and I told her, 'I love you, but I don't buy what you are telling me.'"

Captivated by murder charges filed after three months of anticipation, the national media also was eager for the sheriff and family members to talk. Producers with NBC's Today Show called Ann

Danison and coaxed her to answer questions about her feelings towards her daughter. She reluctantly agreed. Massey was surprised on Dec. 11 that his live interview with Today Show co-host Matt Lauer included a split screen shared with Amanda's mom.

Danison was asked first if she believed in her heart that her daughter was capable of murdering the children.

"Well, I would've never thought so, but you know, by what the evidence shows to be different, I hate to think that," she told the Today Show audience. "I decided from the very beginning what the investigators came up with, that's what I was going to go along with and that's what they've come up with."

She said Amanda was a devoted mother who spent all her time with her children. "I never would have dreamed in a million years that she would do something like this. She knows I would've taken the kids."

Lauer asked about Amanda's mental stability.

"She's had her problems throughout her childhood. Low self-esteem. She's had a lot of problems in her life."

And what about Maurice's relationship with the children?

"Well, I always thought he was great. He played basketball with the boys. I thought he was attached to Kyleigh. I wasn't crazy about the relationship, only because he couldn't hold a job. Amanda was the one supporting him. He couldn't watch the kids while she was working, so I did not approve of the relationship. But I accepted it because I wanted to make sure I could see the kids."

Lauer asked the sheriff only three questions, first why the drownings were now considered murders.

"Well, we think we're going to be able to quickly prove that this was not an accident and that it was an intentional act, and we believe we can hold both of them accountable for this," said Massey.

"What bothers you the most about their version of the events of Sept. 2?" Lauer asked.

"Their version would indicate that it was an accident, like you mentioned. We've done extensive vehicle testing with the same vehicle back at the lake. We've consulted with medical specialists. We've done literally hundreds of interviews that I think will quickly contradict that theory," said Massey.

The sheriff also side-stepped Lauer's question about a possible motive, saying the state would present that information in court. "But we do have a motive and I think the jury will take a quick look at it and agree with us." Massey seemed confident.

As Lauer wrapped up the interview, Ann asked to add one last comment:

"I just want to express how grateful I am to Roger Massey, Rick Hawn, Sergeant Halloran, all the investigators, the people that helped try to save my kids, my grandkids. They've been wonderful and I'm grateful for that," she said.

What was already the highest profile court case in DeWitt County's history was about to also become the most expensive for its taxpayers and most time consuming for lawyers assigned to handle it.

Chapter Sixteen

The effort to ensure justice is carried out has a couple things in common with brain surgery. First, it's no time to cut corners budget-wise. There's no greater justification than a potential death penalty for defense lawyers to have all the resources they need.

That's why the State of Illinois set up a Capital Litigation Trust Fund in 1999 so counties lacking deep pockets could fund high costs associated with murder cases. Defendants were allowed two qualified lawyers and an investigator to help chase down information, confer with experts, conduct interviews and anything else needed to equal the state's legion of tax-supported prosecutors, experts and investigators.

Another thing justice has in common with life-saving surgery is the reluctance most people have to ask about the price. But elected politicians who feel a duty to keep their eyes on public purse strings will probe where others are reluctant.

A week after ink was dry on the murder charges, DeWitt County Board Chairman Duane Harris, a soft-spoken phone company retiree, said he was researching the potential cost of the two capital cases. He believed it was almost certain to exceed the $100,000 the county had in a contingency fund to cover extra legal costs.

Sheriff Massey let it be known there would be no cost estimates coming from him. "This investigation is not driven by costs," he said.

The state required counties to spend their own resources before tapping state coffers. The fact that the special prosecutor Roger Simpson was not on the county's payroll was a unique element of the case; the state trust fund might step in to pay his salary.

Simpson would be assisted by Ed Parkinson, a state government employee in the state appellate prosecutor's office. The county routinely paid Parkinson's office a flat annual fee of $7,500 for legal services. With the double murder case looming, it looked like a real bargain.

On Dec. 18, Simpson and Parkinson laid out the evidence for members of a DeWitt County grand jury. Massey, Halloran, Hawn and Greg Lindenmulder, a state police detective, were all witnesses in the closed-door proceeding.

Massey went through the timeline of the incident, emphasizing why he formed early doubts about Maurice's version of what happened. The sheriff closed his testimony with statements made to police Sept. 17 and 18 when Amanda accused Maurice of being abusive to her and the children.

Halloran was next in the grand jury room. His testimony centered on the interview with Amanda at St. Mary's Hospital following her lie detector test there. The nods Amanda made in agreement to police questions about what she may have known about Maurice's plans to harm her children were described to grand jurors.

Halloran also testified how Maurice's voice can be heard on the 911 call only seconds after Amanda began the call.

Lindenmulder's role was to summarize reports from Deputy Tim Collins, including information about the moisture content of Amanda's clothing and hair. Amanda's sweat pants were soaked and heavy to the point of falling down, but her white t-shirt did not appear to be wet, according to Collins' observation passed along by Lindenmulder. Her shoulder-length hair appeared to be "blowing in the wind," something not likely if her hair were dripping wet, according to the testimony.

Detective Hawn was the final witness. He offered his conclusions that with the exception of it being water-logged, the car was operating properly when it was pulled from the water.

The grand jury quickly returned murder indictments that mirrored charges filed days earlier. A public preliminary hearing on the evidence had been avoided, just as prosecutors had hoped.

At a brief hearing on Christmas Eve, Maurice told Judge Peters he had been unable to hire a lawyer. The news was not unanticipated; the judge immediately appointed two Decatur lawyers to represent Maurice. The judge chose the pair for their experience and proximity to Clinton.

Jeff Justice and Tom Griffith had worked together on three previous murder cases. Both were former prosecutors who went on to separate private practices. Justice, named lead counsel, had flamboyance and bravado when it came to taking issue with matters inside a courtroom. He brushed off banter about his fondness for purple shirts and ties.

Griffith, his partner on Maurice's case, was equally passionate about his work but more reserved, a temperament that served him well in the future. He would be named a judge eight years later. He often joked about the challenge of getting sufficient sleep in a household where he and his wife were raising two sets of twins, the first pair still toddlers.

Both defense lawyers were experienced members of the local bar—Justice with 24 years and Griffith 17 years. Both stood tall and lanky, several inches above their client.

Amanda's legal team gained a second lawyer with the appointment of Springfield lawyer D. Peter Wise to assist Skelton. The private practice lawyer, who would serve as a publicly-funded attorney in the DeWitt County case, had handled other murder cases in his 16 years of law practice.

The first week of the new year saw Maurice and Amanda back in court, at separate hearings, to enter not guilty pleas. The courtroom was packed with media and family members.

Amanda trembled as she sat between Skelton and Wise. Maurice appeared calm at his hearing.

Poised with microphones, video and still cameras, reporters waited outside the courtroom for any relative or lawyer willing to talk. Maurice LaGrone Sr. broke his public silence as he returned to the courthouse lobby after occupying a front row seat at both hearings.

"They're both innocent," Maurice's father declared. "They've done nothing wrong. They loved those kids." He called the charges "ridiculous" and said they would be disproved when the truth came out.

The seven reporters who would cover the cases from start to finish were happy the prosecution's Parkinson and all four defense lawyers were willing to speak to them, providing sure-fire fodder for their stories. But Simpson, the lead prosecutor bound by state Supreme Court rules requiring him to avoid disclosing evidence ahead of a trial, routinely left court without speaking to the media.

What became common practice after each court date was for a lawyer from one side to answer reporters' questions while the other side observed from the sidelines. Sometimes the remarks were a layman's explanation of what had just occurred in court. Other times the attorneys offered fiery reaction to their competitor's approach to justice.

Wise took the first swing after his first court appearance with Amanda.

"We believe there is a compelling, righteous and gripping story to be told here, and we'll do it as well as we know how," he said.

Parkinson, a prosecutor with more than 70 murder trials under his belt, took exception and returned the punch.

"I don't know what he means by 'righteous.' For most people, it's almost unbelievable that three innocent children would lose their lives in the way we—the state—believes they did. We feel that we have a case that will bring these people to justice."

Parkinson said the state would fight any defense effort to move trials outside DeWitt County. Jurors may be taken to the scene of the incident during the state's case, he said.

Still to be settled by prosecutors were two issues: Would Amanda and Maurice be tried separately or together? And would the state seek the death penalty?

April 4 was the deadline set for a capital punishment decision.

Chapter Seventeen

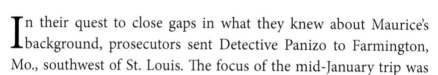

In their quest to close gaps in what they knew about Maurice's background, prosecutors sent Detective Panizo to Farmington, Mo., southwest of St. Louis. The focus of the mid-January trip was the June 2000 death of Maurice's infant son, Dorshawn.

Authorities in Farmington felt confident no foul play was indicated in the death of the 2-month-old as he slept in bed between his parents.

Back in DeWitt County, the state won court permission to open several bags of Maurice's possessions Clinton police had retrieved from Amanda's apartment when she asked officers to accompany her home to remove his belongings.

The contents of a black leather bag and three trash bags stored for months at the sheriff's department might offer insights into the couple's relationship, prosecutors had argued. "The investigation has revealed that LaGrone was rarely employed and was essentially financed by Amanda Hamm and that Hamm often purchased expensive clothing and jewelry for LaGrone," Massey wrote in court documents for the warrants.

Specifically, police were looking for photos, jewelry, bank records and receipts for the Sunset Inn, the Clinton motel where Maurice and Amanda went swimming.

Items collected from the search warrant would be another piece in the puzzle investigators were putting together for a future jury. If jurors could be convinced Maurice was a lazy boyfriend able to control his vulnerable girlfriend and persuade her to buy him gifts with her hard-earned money, the idea that he was selfish enough to kill three nuisance children would be less difficult to convey. The state's theory was supported by contents of the leather bag: pricey shoes and pants beyond the financial reach of a dishwasher.

Police were trying to take a deep dive into Maurice's conduct with Amanda and her children and his life before the two had met. His disappointing performance as a young adult gave police plenty of ammunition, and it was all fair game. Even so, Maurice's tight-lipped stance had made it difficult for police and prosecutors to piece together a motive for murder.

Meanwhile, family members in St. Louis and Bloomington supported him. They didn't press him for details about the drownings, instead relying on what they knew of him—a good-natured prankster who loved spending time with his cousins.

Amanda's support network was thin, consisting mainly of medical staff and counselors paid to help her with her grief. But it added an important new member when her mother returned to her side.

Ann Danison's view of the case shifted as she learned from Steve Skelton about the state's evidence and how it was gathered. She visited her daughter in jail.

"She's still my daughter," she told a reporter in February. "And I still love her."

Chapter Eighteen

The possibility that Amanda and Maurice could be executed if convicted was a constant ingredient of public discourse about the drownings. Concerned the continuing debate could distract from the questions of guilt or innocence, the state announced in late January it did not plan to seek the death penalty in either case.

The no-capital punishment decision meant an immediate loss of Wise and Griffith from the defense teams and a shift of the total financial burden for the cases to DeWitt County taxpayers. The connection between money and justice was an unavoidable reality for the small town; people knew the cases would be resolved at some point but the financial consequences could last for years.

Prosecutors retained a right to revisit the death penalty decision as the cases moved closer to trial.

A fresh estimate that the twin murder cases could shrink DeWitt County coffers by $1 million or more put public officials on the defensive. When bills began arriving at the treasurer's office, county board members began to vent.

"It sounds harsh when you're talking about people's lives and justice and then you talk about money, but why weren't the people who have to foot the bill talked to?" asked Ed Young, the county board's finance chairman.

In the wake of negative comments by local officials, Justice let it be known lawyers for the two defendants were looking for ways to economize when appropriate, sharing information and research common to both cases. Justice vowed to try to limit the cost of Maurice's defense to $350,000—still a far distance from the $45,000 the county had available in its current budget for court-appointed attorneys. The pledge from Justice did little to smooth choppy waters.

"We don't have any idea how much this stupid trial is going to cost us," county board member Chris Riddle complained during a mid-March meeting. "Somebody should be smart enough to tell us how much it's going to cost."

Amanda's mother was quick to criticize Riddle's remark.

"It's unfortunate the county board will suffer the financial loss of paying for the 'stupid trials' but when compared to the loss of three young lives and their families, how can the county board put a price tag on the cost of justice?" Danison said in a statement.

Dave Hamm, one of Christopher's uncles, concurred. "We don't want any mistakes. We want justice no matter what," he said.

To further justify legal costs, Justice told the county its financial obligation included about $1,500 for a survey of local residents to determine if they had pre-formed opinions about the murder cases. In his request for the study, Justice noted only 84 blacks lived in all of DeWitt County.

Meanwhile mid-April developments inside and outside the courtroom suggested the death penalty could be back on the table. The first clue came when Skelton asked that a second lawyer be returned to his team, something he was entitled to only in a capital case.

With Maurice's trial set for late October, Skelton was putting long hours into preparation of Amanda's case in anticipation of her trial soon after that. One room of his Bloomington office was now devoted to her case.

Three days after Skelton's request, the death penalty was indeed back in play.

A handful of federal inmates who had spent time in the DeWitt County jail with Maurice were giving investigators potential evidence that, if true, made prosecutors feel death seemed like the right punishment for both defendants. Detectives were excited about the incriminating statements that included material they had not heard from other sources.

Justice predicted the state's reversal about the death penalty would delay Maurice's trial because he and his fellow defense lawyers would now have the added burden of preparing for a possible sentencing hearing where the outcome could be an execution.

"The case up until Friday was about guilt or innocence," he said. "Now, the jury will be considering the appropriate punishment. It involves everything from the day of his birth until he was arrested."

The distasteful link between justice and money was not raised again publicly, but county officials breathed a quiet sigh of relief. Reinstatement of the possible death penalty meant legal bills would again be forwarded to the state government.

Chapter Nineteen

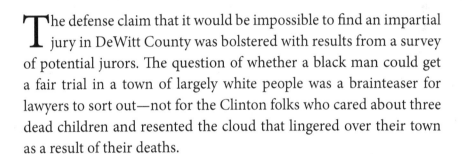

The defense claim that it would be impossible to find an impartial jury in DeWitt County was bolstered with results from a survey of potential jurors. The question of whether a black man could get a fair trial in a town of largely white people was a brainteaser for lawyers to sort out—not for the Clinton folks who cared about three dead children and resented the cloud that lingered over their town as a result of their deaths.

Maurice's legal team attached the survey findings to its motion to move the trial outside the county.

The survey team reached nearly 1,100 households from a list of 12,515 potential jurors. Nearly 800 had agreed to answer more questions after they acknowledged knowing something about the case. More than half deemed Maurice likely guilty of murder.

Only six said he was probably innocent.

About the same percentage considered Amanda to be guilty of killing her children.

The vast majority of those polled cited news accounts and conversations with friends as their main sources of information about the drownings. The county was saturated with details of the accident, Justice argued, including gossip spread by people with lifelong connections to the victims' families.

People had seen Amanda's mother on national television saying her daughter should be punished for her part in the deaths, and they were aware of local officials' handwringing over trial costs. That was just the start of the negative influences that would likely impact jury selection, Justice argued.

The sheriff's comparison of the case to the Susan Smith murders of her sons also could not be erased from memories of local residents who might be called to the jury box, the defense said.

The broadcast remarks from the sheriff and Amanda's mother—people with knowledge of the case—by themselves were sufficient to convince Judge Peters to move the trial to Champaign, 40 miles away. "This separates them from ordinary opinion," the judge said in his ruling.

In late June, prosecutors said they wanted to try Maurice and Amanda together. A trial date in the following spring had already been set for Amanda— on April 4, her 28th birthday. Now, if the state had its way, Maurice would face the same jury on the same day.

On Aug. 25, for the first time since their arrests eight months earlier, Maurice and Amanda sat in the same courtroom while their attorneys argued for separate trials outside DeWitt County.

The former lovers' eyes never met. Maurice stared at the table in front of him for most of the two-hour hearing. Amanda focused on her lawyers.

Statements from Maurice and Amanda about how the car went into the lake were consistent and not antagonistic, Parkinson argued in his motion for a joint trial. He said separate trials were unnecessary because the state lacked confessions from either defendant implicating themselves or others.

"They were together when the children drowned. This can be done once instead of twice," he said.

For his initial review of what Maurice and Amanda had said to police, the judge was given 16 pages of statements, sealed.

D. Peter Wise, who returned to the defense team after the case became a potential death penalty matter again, noted how Amanda's statements changed in the weeks after the drownings.

"Those statements will condemn Mr. LaGrone. Mrs. Hamm's defense will be greatly antagonistic against Mr. LaGrone," he said. It was the first public hint of a divide between the co-defendants in their explanations of how the children had died.

The judge ruled separate trials were needed, saying disagreements existed between Amanda and Maurice, that a single trial "could be a battle between the defendants and not between the state and an individual defendant."

Maurice and Amanda were now locked into individual struggles to avoid a murder conviction that could result in lethal injection.

As the first anniversary of the drownings approached, every news outlet in the area prepared fresh coverage. Television crews and print media were in town and on the phone gathering comments from relatives, friends and police. There was agreement that if time heals all wounds, a year had been insufficient to mend those inflicted on the community.

A waitress at Grecian Gardens told reporters she hoped the children would not be forgotten as the spotlight turned towards their mother and her ex-boyfriend. Amanda's mother joined others in marking the anniversary with a memorial ceremony at a local park. Mounds of flowers again marked the three graves.

The media reached a deal with lawyers over access to information kept under wraps in closed meetings with the judge. Reporters would have access to legal motions, but supporting documents would be sealed. If attorneys wanted to seal a motion, a hearing would be held to allow the media to state its position.

With defense documents now available, the public was about to learn a lot more about evidence the state planned to use against Maurice and Amanda.

The first the public learned of Amanda's psychiatric treatment at the Decatur hospital and her fateful interview with police there was in a motion filed by her lawyers.

"Throughout the interrogation, these police officers used deceit, deception, trickery and other coercive tactics to exploit Amanda Hamm's personal characteristics as well as her suicidal and depressed mental state," lawyers claimed in their motion to keep the statements from a jury.

In January 2005—now 16 months since the deaths–Tom Griffith and a lawyer with the death penalty trial assistance division of the Illinois Appellate Defender's Office conducted a mock trial of Maurice's case. The goal was to determine each side's strengths and weaknesses before the case played out in front of an actual jury.

"Mock" jurors, hired by a marketing research firm, reported to a Bloomington hotel for their make-believe jury duty. Defense lawyers played the part of the defense, prosecution and judge for the staged trial.

The pretend jury heard Maurice tell his side of the story through the videotaped interview police conducted at the lake, an interview Maurice's actual jury would never see. The mock jury also did not hear testimony about Amanda's interview with police while she was a psychiatric patient.

Maurice was acquitted after 20 minutes of deliberation by the mock panel. With a cautionary note from his lawyers that the exercise was strictly a tool for trial preparation, Maurice was informed of the mock verdict. The public would not learn of the practice run until after the real trial was concluded.

In March, Amanda's lawyers received a delay in her April trial, saying more time was needed to coordinate the extensive list of witnesses they planned to call. They included experts in accident reconstruction, mechanical and automotive engineering and locking systems as well as psychiatrists, psychologists and sociologists.

Meanwhile Maurice's lawyers said he and his defense team were ready to face a jury. "We spoke to our client and, after a year and a half in jail, he's ready," said Justice. Maurice's trial would start May 2.

First there would be court decisions on what testimony and evidence jurors would be allowed to hear and see. The reality of a courtroom showdown began to sink in.

Chapter Twenty

Criminal cases frequently are won or lost before the jury even enters the courtroom. It's at pre-trial hearings the judge decides, based on relevance and fairness, what evidence can be presented and what testimony jurors will be allowed to hear. The defense teams representing Amanda Hamm and Maurice LaGrone had exhaustive challenges ready to what prosecutors wanted to present jurors—all of it damaging to the two defendants.

But even before those arguments would begin, there was the matter of whether the jury should be taken to the lake during Maurice's trial for a firsthand look at the scene. The defense opposed the state's request for the field trip.

"What's troubling from our viewpoint is the uncontrolled nature of this," said Justice.

The notion that jurors would step off a bus near the boat ramp and then be free to take in all the sites surrounding the scene was an extremely troubling proposition for the defense. How could they be certain jurors were not making unknown and unwarranted assumptions based on what they saw?

But prosecutors wanted to give jurors the first-hand experience, a chance to envision how far the car had drifted from shore and just how close the two adults were to the vehicle as it sank. The circumstances—and yes, the drama—of three children going down with the car could be much better perceived at the water's edge than in a courtroom, with a pointer and poster, Parkinson argued.

Even the words used to describe the place were an issue for the two sides.

The defense motion filed in opposition to the lake visit curiously referred to the boat ramp area as a "crime scene," as opposed to the scene of an accident, a distinction Parkinson couldn't help but applaud.

"We appreciate them saying that," he quipped during the hearing. If it were an accident, he told Judge Peters, no trial would be needed.

The judge decided there would be no visit to the lake. The state had not persuaded him that jurors needed to stand on its shore to clarify images they would see in photos and videos presented in the courtroom.

Maurice's lawyers filed a stack of eight motions related to statements they wanted to keep from a jury. They covered everything from negative assessments by Kyleigh's father of Amanda's parenting skills to rumors heard by three women about alleged physical abuse of the children by Maurice.

What family and acquaintances thought of the couple's relationship and how it changed after the deaths was another area defense lawyers didn't want the state to explore with a jury.

"These witnesses are trying to interpret the emotions of two people who have gone through a traumatic event and make conclusions as to how LaGrone and Hamm should have reacted under those circumstances," Justice argued.

Conclusions based on observations by people in the margins of Amanda's and Maurice's lives were a looming hazard for both defense teams. The smallest recollections suddenly had the potential to be blockbuster evidence.

Some of the pending testimony contained such potentially prejudicial material that even the titles of the motions weren't being publicly disclosed.

"The very subject of the motion—the title of the information I seek to bar—gives away what I want you to rule as inadmissible," said Justice.

He asked that his motion about testimony concerning Maurice's "character attributes" be kept secret. Going a step further to contain any leaks of information, Justice asked that the courtroom be cleared for a hearing on Amanda's statement and the reliability of a jailhouse informant.

Justice compared the information he wanted kept out of the courtroom to "calling someone a member of al-Qaida or the KKK."

Despite objections from the media, Judge Peters allowed the lawyers to air their arguments behind closed doors. He ruled some of the negative material about Maurice and statements by others about the children would be allowed at the trial.

The potential role of science in the trials came into focus with the state's attempt to introduce 10 tests performed on the car and defense lawyers' efforts to find an expert who could address those findings.

Just less than a month before the scheduled start of Maurice's trial, his lawyers told the judge they weren't ready to proceed with the May 2 date. A critical meeting with an automotive expert was given by Justice as the reason for the delay.

Sitting between his lawyers in the courtroom, Maurice answered the judge's questions in soft tones, confirming he understood the request for a postponement.

The judge agreed to the delay, cautioning the lawyers that if a trial were not started by October, it would likely be pushed into 2006 because of the holidays.

The scientific evidence many people were anticipating focused on how long the children were in the water before they were rescued. The answer could support or demolish the veracity of Amanda's initial statements.

Dr. Kris Bysani, the Peoria doctor who treated Kyleigh, was expected to testify for the state that the toddler had been underwater

30 to 40 minutes—more than double the estimates made by Amanda. He based his opinion on the child's low body temperature.

A competing opinion would come from Dr. Daniel Schultz. A forensic pathologist from Florida hired by the defense, he was prepared to testify Kyleigh's resuscitation would have been unlikely if she had been underwater for more than 10 minutes.

The judge ruled jurors could hear from both doctors and decide for themselves which opinion to accept.

Simpson told the judge the state planned to call Amanda as a witness in Maurice's trial. The state was willing to offer her "use immunity," protecting her from having her statements at Maurice's trial later used against her in her own trial. She could still exercise her constitutional right against self-incrimination, though the judge could order her to testify.

The location of Maurice's trial was moved a second time after Champaign County backed away from hosting the trial because no courtroom was available for the lengthy trial now that it was delayed. Instead, it would be held in Bloomington, in McLean County, 25 miles north of Clinton and where Maurice had lived.

The defense said a McLean County survey taken to measure potential jurors' familiarity with the case found 75 percent of those asked knew something about the case and 60 percent believed the defendants were probably guilty.

The defense wanted still another trial site to be found. Judge Peters rejected that request and scheduled Maurice's trial for February of 2006.

With what was expected to be a six-week trial finally in sight, Roger Massey took a short break from the investigation to announce he would seek a fourth term as sheriff.

Maurice, meanwhile, had been jailed 21 months, awaiting his day in court. "My job is to be a good inmate," he told Justice, "and not cause any trouble that could affect my case and be patient."

As the trial date neared, transcripts of some of the closed-door hearings became available to the media. In a May hearing, prosecutors had revealed a motive.

"What we're trying to show is the motive for Maurice LaGrone to eliminate these bothersome kids from his daily self-pleasure of smoking marijuana, having sex, not working, living off his girlfriend," Parkinson had told the court. "That's his life."

"Motive is not character assassination," Justice told reporters, and the fact that Maurice cheated on his girlfriend and failed to keep a steady job did not make him a murderer. The state, he said, was going too far in trashing Maurice's character in its effort to convict him.

With the trial only weeks away, Maurice's legal team felt obligated to share with their client the reality that things could go badly at a high stakes trial. An offer from Maurice to plead guilty to reckless homicide in return for a 28-year sentence—the maximum allowed for the charge—was sternly rejected by prosecutor Simpson.

Chapter Twenty-one

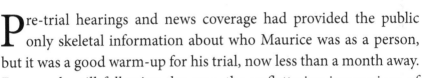

Pre-trial hearings and news coverage had provided the public only skeletal information about who Maurice was as a person, but it was a good warm-up for his trial, now less than a month away. For people still following the case, the unflattering impressions of Maurice were starting to meld into an image of a child killer.

On Clinton streets, some residents seemed as anxious as the lawyers and defendants to get the trials started. Others just wanted it over. The possibility that Maurice and Amanda could face death if convicted added a layer to community conversation.

The debate took on two opposing tones that always resonate when people try to justify or eliminate capital punishment as an appropriate punishment: Taking a life is all right if it evens a score; and two wrongs don't make a right.

Two weeks before the start of Maurice's trial, the Coalition for Non-Violent Communities, a group newly formed to address social justice issues in central Illinois, sponsored a town hall meeting in Clinton to give people a chance to air their feelings about the death penalty. About two dozen people attended the session at a local church. Among them was Amanda's mother.

Capital punishment was not something she thought about before it became an issue for her daughter, Ann Danison admitted to an audience heavily weighted with supporters of the death penalty. Ultimately, the decision to end a life rests with God, she said.

"If God can forgive, who are we to make the decision to kill somebody?" she asked the group.

Forgiveness is all well and good, one person responded in a respectful tone, but justice sometimes calls for the ultimate penalty.

On Feb. 21, 2006—903 days after the tragedy at the lake—jury selection began in the largest courtroom in the McLean County Law and Justice Center. With room for about 75 spectators, the more spacious setting seemed to add gravity to the case, if anything could be more fateful than a capital murder case. Ann Danison and her sister sat in the back row. Two of the children's fathers were also there.

For the first time since his arrest, Maurice, now 30, came to court wearing something other than a jail uniform. Dressed in a gray sweater and slacks and a white dress shirt provided by Jeff Justice, he looked like he could be on his way to an office job. Throughout the trial, he would wear shirts that covered tattoos on his neck, lest they steer jurors toward notions of gangs and a thug lifestyle.

The inked images of a musical note and his nickname "Reece" had no sinister connections, but the defense was taking no chances with what jurors might think.

Judge Peters had set aside two weeks for jury selection and used a process that virtually guaranteed it would take that long to choose 12 jurors and four alternates. Jury candidates came from a group of 250 randomly-selected McLean County residents.

The selection process started with a group of 24 brought into the courtroom. The judge introduced the attorneys, who stood and greeted jurors, and then Maurice, who stood and nodded an acknowledgement to the jury box.

Peters read a list of about 70 names of people who could be witnesses—about 40 for the state and 30 for the defense—to determine if any of the potential jurors were acquainted with them.

The judge explained the fundamental facts of the case and the charges, then gave jurors the trial's basic blueprint: First a determination of guilt or innocence and, if Maurice were convicted, the jury would decide if he was eligible for the death penalty. A finding that Maurice was a candidate for death would mean jurors would then have to decide whether he should be executed.

The group was returned to a jury assembly room and then brought back to the open courtroom one-by-one for individual interviews, first by the judge, then the attorneys.,

A retiree from State Farm, Bloomington's dominant employer, was the first person to be questioned and the first to be excused after he told the judge he was unable to set aside an opinion. Also of concern was the man's fishing trip a week earlier near the west side boat ramp at Clinton Lake.

One woman who was ultimately excused expressed the heavy burden the death penalty placed on jurors.

"It would cause me a lot of sleepless nights," she said. "I would wonder if I was doing the right thing," said the black woman, fighting back tears as she imagined what the final hours of deliberation could hold.

After the judge's 45-minute inquiry of each person, the lawyers had their own questions.

What about bi-racial relationships? Jeff Justice asked a woman.

"It's a lot more prevalent than when I was growing up. You love the people who you love. It's not for me to decide," the potential juror, a white woman, answered.

Life experiences were important too. Any specific, water-related trauma was relevant for lawyers, whether it involved swimming, boating or driving through a flooded street.

Justice acknowledged the 500-pound elephant in the room with his inquiry about the lengths parents would go to save their children. "If those were my kids in the car, I'd die trying to save them," the defense attorney said, echoing the sentiments of many.

A father of two children the same ages as Christopher and Austin gave Justice an equally honest reply.

"When the judge described the charges, the first thing on my mind was my kids in the back seat. I'd do anything to get them out," he said before being excused.

So, after eight days of questions for a total of 58 people, and input from Maurice to his lawyers, the defense and prosecution settled on a jury of five men and seven women. Half of them were connected to State Farm, as were three of the four alternates. Two of the main jurors and one alternate were black.

With the selection process complete, jurors were sent home for a few days while lawyers wrapped up a series of pre-trial hearings. The jurors were told to avoid any news coverage of the case.

The arsenal of weapons available to the state to convict Maurice grew larger and more lethal at the pre-trial hearings. Judge Peters ruled prosecutors would be allowed to tell the jury about statements made by Amanda during her 19-day hospital stay—assuming she could be persuaded to testify at Maurice's trial.

The courtroom debate over her potential testimony was the first time there was a public airing of the accusations police said they gathered at the psychiatric unit interview. Justice unsuccessfully argued Amanda's statements were made under the influence of multiple psychiatric medications and therefore unreliable.

"I think she would have said she killed John Kennedy that day," Justice told the judge.

In a ruling that would give the defense some muscle to challenge the state's assault on Maurice's character, the judge agreed several of Maurice's former girlfriends could testify about their relationships with him and his behavior around their children.

Simpson objected to the testimony. "Prior good conduct is not relevant to this case," he said. Tom Griffith challenged Simpson, offering a different view of romantic break-ups that never turned violent.

"This pattern shows that when things got tough, Maurice LaGrone didn't kill the kids. He left," Griffith argued.

Three days before the trial was to begin, Maurice was returned to Clinton and his DeWitt County jail cell. The four lawyers spent the long weekend preparing for weeks of grueling courtroom work. All five men were eager and apprehensive.

Chapter Twenty-two

It was hard to find an empty seat in the large courtroom. Members of Maurice's family settled into two rows, having made the trip from the St. Louis area through severe spring-like weather, even though winter's end was technically still a week away on this March 13, 2006.

Twice as many people in the courtroom had a connection to Amanda or the children. Their commute was generally short, but their interest was high. They knew what happened in Maurice's case could very well impact the outcome of the next trial. News organizations had 14 people present to report on opening statements.

With jurors in their places, quiet cloaked the courtroom as the special prosecutor, Roger Simpson, stepped to the podium. His tone was friendly and confident. He said there was nothing mysterious about the deaths of Christopher, Austin and Kyleigh. "This is not a 'whodunit,'" he said. "This is a 'how' case." And there were consequences attached.

Simpson shared a backyard baseball story from his youth, a tale of what can happen when a boy's lucky enough to have his bat make contact with his older brother's pitch. He didn't mean to hit the ball through the window of a neighbor's house. But the reckless result, a shattered glass, still bore consequences.

In Simpson's mind, his careless homer had something in common with Maurice's bravado on a boat ramp: Both actions carried the strong probability of serious harm, one to a window, the other to three small children. One of the nine murder counts against Maurice accused him of causing the car to go into the water, an act that held every possibility of harm to its backseat passengers. Left unsaid by the prosecutor was the fact that his careless long ball didn't have lethal injection as a potential consequence.

Circumstances surrounding the trip to the lake that fateful September evening would prove the couple had plotted to kill the children, Simpson told jurors. The situation in Amanda's household had changed for the worse soon after Amanda's new boyfriend moved in, he said, Maurice being cruel to the children and Amanda powerless to stop the abuse.

"She was frightened. She was controlled. She was scared. She had been abused," said the prosecutor, now breaking from the state's longstanding characterization of Amanda as a co-conspirator and anything but a victim.

Maurice liked marijuana and a woman's full attention, Simpson continued.

"There will be testimony that he took pride in that he could control white women."

He said the state would prove through scientific evidence that the car was fully functional, even though it was in the water.

"In short, the evidence will show that there is no earmark from the physical evidence that this was an accident at all."

Simpson told jurors they would learn how Amanda and Maurice shared a shower at her mother's house only hours after the children died, and how Maurice was heard to tell his girlfriend, "We've got to get our stories straight."

How Maurice convinced Amanda to go along with killing her children was "a study of human behavior," the prosecutor continued.

"This tragedy grew out of a dysfunctional relationship, a woman who was torn between wanting a man and protecting her children and herself."

As Simpson's hour-long opening argument drew to a close, he challenged jurors to keep common sense close at hand as they weighed evidence. Any person who's ever driven a car, he suggested, was familiar with the need to be able to stop a vehicle in a dangerous situation.

Simpson said he was confident jurors would be true to their oath and "true to the concept that we are here to do justice for our community. For our citizens. For ourselves. For the fathers of these three children. And the three children themselves.

"Being true to your oath, doing justice," he said, "will require a verdict of guilty."

It would take Tom Griffith about twice as long to preview defense arguments in a case he called "extremely, exceedingly difficult." Griffith conceded the enormity of the tragedy could lead to an inclination to convict Maurice despite defense evidence that the deaths were an accident.

"I mean the car is in the water. Three children are dead. Somebody has to pay. Guilty!"

Griffith's voice took on a timbre of blunt truth and desperation. "And to be frank with you, that's our biggest hurdle in defending our client."

But one very important thing was missing from the state's case, Griffith said: motive. In most cases where children die at the hands of an adult, there is money or some other reward in the offing. In this case, it was just the opposite. The children were a conduit of money and housing helpfully provided them through public assistance—not to mention child support payments from their fathers. Maurice benefited from the children's very existence.

Griffith stepped away from the podium, moving to the edge of the jury box. The intimacy was not lost on jurors, who were paying close attention to his lengthy recitation of the life events that had brought his client into this courtroom. Maurice was not a murderer, Griffith said, but he was plenty of other things.

He was a high school dropout who held 31 jobs between ages 18 and 28. When problems developed with girlfriends, he hit the road. He was a bit of a mooch.

Maurice's unstable and nomadic life as a teenager—23 household moves over 10 years—did not create a model partner for an equally traumatized single woman with three children. And the notion that Maurice was the mastermind behind a murder plot made no sense, Griffith argued.

"The guy who allegedly planned this incident is the same guy who got demoted at the Coastal Station in Clinton because he could not operate a cash register and he could not count change. They had to demote him to stock boy."

Griffith informed jurors they'd have the opportunity to hear from Maurice himself about what happened at the lake that day.

"Maurice will tell you that versus hitting the brakes, which obviously he should have done, it was like he was caught in a snow bank, and he was going to gun it, gun it, gun it, to get out of that snow bank."

Griffith paused and looked at the jurors. His tone shifted. "And if he had braked, I wouldn't be standing here, ladies and gentlemen."

Griffith cautioned jurors there would be much to sort out from witness statements, starting with the sheriff's conclusion within 90 minutes of the tragedy that a crime had taken place. There would be experts describing how cars function after they have been submerged in water and how people handle grief.

Opening statements had lasted three hours. Jurors were taken to a nearby restaurant for an extended lunch break. When they returned, they would hear from the prosecution's first witness in a parade of people with unflattering stories to tell about Maurice and Amanda.

Chapter Twenty-three

The state is not required to provide a jury with a motive for a crime. But jurors generally want to understand why a crime took place in addition to who was responsible and how it occurred. Prosecutors fear that when there's no clear motive, particularly when the defense claims it was all an accident, jurors might well acquit.

And so the state's first witness, Sally Nichols, a late entry in this legal drama, told the jury about a conversation she had with Amanda in 2003 about Maurice.

"She said she didn't know what she was going to do because her new boyfriend didn't like kids," said Nichols, whose son had worked at a restaurant with Amanda.

Her advice to Amanda? "Get rid of the boyfriend."

In his cross examination, Griffith asked Nichols about when she first told police about that conversation. Almost two and a half years had passed between Amanda's remark about Maurice and Nichols' interview with the sheriff, she said—a meeting arranged after she had talked with a couple of sheriff's department staffers.

Yes, the defense had highlighted the long delay. But the state had made its point.

Kim Gaff had known Amanda for 15 years and worked closely with her and her children in Gaff's role as an early childhood educator, a school district worker who helped children prepare for school and monitor their progress through home visits.

She eagerly shared her opinion about Amanda's relationship with Maurice and the effect his arrival had on the household.

"Amanda was a single parent with very young children and was certainly experiencing single parenthood in full bloom," she said in a long monologue about the challenges Amanda faced and what Gaff did to help.

She told jurors Amanda was missing appointments with her for home visits, partly because she was working two jobs to keep up with household expenses.

"I noticed that Amanda did not look me in the eye anymore when she talked," she said. And there was more.

"There definitely was a change in the children when Mr. LaGrone moved into the house."

Austin and Kyleigh clung to their mother more and Christopher became extremely protective of Austin at school. The boys shared troubling stories with Gaff about Maurice's behavior with them at home. Gaff said she told Amanda and Ann Danison when Christopher told her Maurice had pushed him down the stairs.

Austin didn't like Maurice because Maurice hit him—an allegation Gaff did not report to child welfare authorities, she said, because she saw no signs of physical abuse.

In his cross-examination, Jeff Justice questioned why the early childhood educator had written file notes about an alleged affair between Maurice and the mother of children in a different family she was also seeing professionally. He lodged repeated objections to Gaff's willingness—to the point of being eager—to offer psychological opinions about the Hamm-LaGrone household, but the judge allowed most of her observations to remain part of the record.

The prosecution needed to remove any thoughts jurors may have that Maurice and Amanda lacked the ability to swim. Three witnesses—the manager of a Clinton motel that made its pool available to non-guests and two sisters who saw the pair swim laps—were called to share their recollections. One of the sisters identified Maurice as a man she had seen at a school playground across the street from her home, shooting baskets with neighborhood kids, Christopher and Austin among them.

Susan Swearingen, the children's babysitter, had also become a sideline observer of the relationship between Amanda and Maurice. Her testimony showed that she had not only kept a mental catalog of what she had seen and heard, but also developed a firm opinion of what it all meant.

Her bottom-line impression was that Amanda was ready to walk, that Amanda was a loving but unskilled mother. Swearingen described Kyleigh's recurring diaper rash and Amanda's consistent failure to buckle the kids in their car seats—just two of the mother's shortcomings Swearingen said she had to remedy on a regular basis.

When Maurice came into the picture, the boys' behavior became less innocent and more combative, Swearingen told the jury. And Kyleigh stopped smiling and giving hugs.

Justice made objection after objection to Swearingen's testimony about what Amanda may have told her about fights with Maurice, most of them over money. Simpson asked whether Amanda ever gave a reason why she didn't ask Maurice to leave?

Before Swearingen could answer, Justice objected once again.

"Judge, the reason has to relate to an issue in this trial," he said. "This isn't a trial about their relationship."

"It *is* a trial about their relationship," Simpson retorted.

Judge Peters stayed the course and allowed the jury to hear Swearingen's answer.

"She said she didn't want to ask him to leave because the sex was great."

Tensions mounted between the lawyers as each side tried to make Swearingen's testimony work for them. When Griffith tried to challenge her recollection of a dispute between Maurice and the boys, Simpson interrupted, suggesting the defense lawyer was not following correct procedure for impeachment of a witness.

"I'll ask a better question to make Mr. Simpson happy," Griffith swatted back.

"I'm not happy or unhappy, Judge. I'm just trying to follow the rules here," said Simpson, his feathers clearly ruffled.

The judge raised the pitch of his normally calm voice.

"Hey. Now if I have to enter an order that the attorneys are not going to speak to one another during the trial, I will do so. I'm asking you please to hold your comments to yourself or else I will enter an order. Proceed," said Peters, agitated at being forced to referee the exchange between lawyers.

Griffith apologized and went on with his questions.

"You don't like Mr. LaGrone. Correct, Mrs. Swearingen?"

"I didn't say that," she said, suppressing the opinion she had offered freely to police three years earlier.

After a full afternoon of testimony, the state had accomplished a goal. The children's babysitter had set the stage for other witnesses' assessment of Maurice's selfishness and Amanda's maternal shortcomings.

Left undetermined was whether the defense had made its point that Swearingen was biased against Maurice. It also wanted jurors to know Swearingen, like Kim Gaff, had not reported the suspected abuse and neglect to child welfare authorities.

Three boys who had been neighbors and friends with the Hamm children looked anxious as they were called one by one to testify. The walk from the courtroom door to the witness stand was a long one. Each boy paused briefly to take in the audience before moving forward to raise his right hand.

The search for another player for an after-school game of kickball at the housing complex the afternoon of the drownings had brought several neighborhood kids within hearing distance of an exchange with Amanda's sons. Two of the boys agreed that it was Christopher who declined an invitation to play because he was "going on a boat ride" with his family. A third witness thought it was Austin who made the statement.

Either way, the state had planted its seed that a trip to the lake may have been planned and talked about well before Christopher, Austin and their little sister climbed into their mother's car.

Chapter Twenty-four

Pam Weikle, the woman who was parked near the boat ramp with her daughter watching for deer, recounted for jurors the concern she felt as a vehicle came speeding toward her car from behind. She was firm in her recollection that a black man was behind the wheel and a small child was behind him.

"He was kind of kneeling against the window, looking over the driver's left shoulder," Weikle said of the boy, whom she described as "mixed race." Whether the onset of dusk at the lake or her certainty that the driver was black led to her mistaken identification of the child as anything other than Caucasian was not explored during questioning.

No one else was in the car, as far as Weikle could tell.

She said the car parked just behind hers near the water, and no one got out while she was there. After she drove off several minutes later, she saw the green car move into her parking spot and then onto the boat ramp before stopping three or four feet from the water's edge. Weikle noticed something unique about damage to the car's trunk. It looked as if it had backed into a pole.

As Weikle left the stand, jurors likely thought back to something Griffith had said in the previous day's opening statement. In every murder trial, he had said, there's one thing that defies explanation.

In this case, he continued, it would be this witness's belief there was only one adult and one child in the car as it approached the lake.

Darren Leggett, the boater who experienced the full brunt of the crisis as he returned from fishing on Clinton Lake, set the scene with his answers to Simpson's questions: A hysterical woman shouting that her kids were dead in a car submerged at the end of the boat ramp. He quoted her as saying the children had been in the car 15 minutes.

As he stood on shore watching rescuers work, Leggett overheard words exchanged between Amanda and Maurice as they watched emergency crews remove the children from the water.

"He was consoling her, saying, 'It will be okay baby, it will be all right.' Something to that effect," Leggett said.

Leggett pushed colored pins onto a large diagram of the lake's West Side Access Area to designate the locations of people and objects. The depiction of the boat ramp and surrounding area was one of many visual aids and photographs lawyers placed on an easel or displayed on a screen to help jurors visualize what they'd hear in testimony.

Every spectator in the courtroom paid close attention to Leggett, the first actual witness to the chaos at the lake to testify.

He acknowledged he was somewhat panicked as he fumbled to find his cell phone in the boat and call 911. But the decision to summon rescue workers seemed the most appropriate course of action, he said—a judgment the defense would later remind jurors was identical to Amanda's panicked race to the pay phone. When Leggett got through to 911, the dispatcher let him know help was already on the way.

"I always thought that was what you were supposed to do, and I didn't know what kind of situation I was getting into."

Justice asked Leggett to explain his concerns.

"A lady is screaming her kids are dead. There's a man in the background. I don't know if it was a violent situation or not. I didn't even pull my boat up to the dock initially. As a matter of fact, I put it in reverse and backed away from the dock," Leggett admitted.

From his vantage point an estimated 200 yards from Maurice and Amanda, Leggett said neither of them appeared wet. He thought Amanda was wearing a skirt.

Next came the recording of the 911 call of Amanda, then Maurice, pleading for help. Sheriff Massey was on the stand to offer supportive information. The tape was played twice. The terms used by most witnesses who described Amanda when they first saw her on the boat ramp—hysterical and out of control—played out on the tape. The jury and spectators sat in frozen silence as voices blared through the courtroom's sound system. Several of the victims' relatives wiped away tears as the dramatic recording took them closer to the tragedy.

Jurors jotted notes as, one by one, first responders took the witness stand and described their efforts to save the children. First was DeWitt County Sheriff's Sergeant Tim Collins, an eight-year veteran of the agency.

He recalled seeing a woman and a man standing near the pay phone and a guy in a boat near the dock. He also saw a car submerged in the water. The woman told him, "My kids are in the car. My babies are in the car."

Collins laid out how the police and paramedics waded into the lake, treading water as necessary, to quickly pull the youngsters from the vehicle. No more than two minutes, he said.

Asked about Amanda's and Maurice's clothing, Collins said Amanda's sweat pants were so wet she struggled to keep them from falling down. He couldn't recall if Maurice's pants were wet.

Discrepancies about how wet or dry Amanda and Maurice's clothing seemed at the lake, the dampness of her hair and whether she was wearing a skirt or pants riddled reports of the first responders who tried to recollect details that paled in comparison to their frantic efforts to save the children.

Collins described how Maurice and Amanda reacted to the traumatic episode after they got out of his squad car at the hospital. Maurice sat with his head in his hands in the waiting room just around the corner from where the children were receiving treatment, Collins remembered.

"They were just babies. It shouldn't have happened to them," Collins quoted Maurice as saying.

And Amanda's state of extreme hysteria persisted as she waited to see her children.

Deputy Bruce Randolph, the second officer to arrive on the scene, testified about his initial assumptions as he surveyed the situation. A boat tied to the dock and a car in the water—another episode involving an incompetent boat owner, he thought. Then he looked closer and realized that what he thought were headlights were actually back-up lights on the car.

The three children were found by touch rather than sight, he testified. "You couldn't see a thing in that water."

Randolph's recollection of the condition of the ramp's surface had changed since the defense took his deposition 15 months earlier (and 15 months after the incident). Now he was saying the ramp didn't seem slippery, different from his earlier statements that moss and algae made the surface quite slick.

Tyrel Klein, the 24-year old correctional officer who went to the lake after hearing the emergency call on his scanner at home, had a similar memory lapse concerning the ramp's surface. Griffith had to help refresh his memory, drawing from the transcript of Klein's earlier interview with lawyers from both sides.

The short trip from the car to the shore with Kyleigh was arduous, Klein had told the lawyers: "I basically crawled out of the water holding the baby above the water using my hands on the grooves of the ramp to pull myself out."

Why, Klein had been asked in that interview, was he crawling?

"It was slick. The moss and the...just the surface of the ramp was slick with my boots and I kept losing my footing."

Now, in the courtroom, Klein came to accept his previous assessment of the ramp. It was slippery.

Emergency Medical Technician Ben Over told the jury that on Sept. 2, 2003, he disregarded training that had taught him to let others handle the rescue while he provided medical care.

"I felt the situation warranted it, and that they needed all the help they could use out at the vehicle," said Over, who had been working with the ambulance crew for about a year in 2003.

Like any first responder rushing to hand off a victim in crisis to emergency room staffers, Over was unable to learn the identity of the child he had tried to revive. The next day a newspaper photo with names of the drowning victims confirmed the child was Austin.

Austin's father Craig Brown wiped tears as he listened to Over's testimony.

Over's partner on the ambulance, Cassandra McFall, had absorbed more details of the lake scene than the other first responders and shared her negative impressions of what she saw. She noticed two people standing near the boat ramp—a male subject standing behind a female subject. And that as she walked past the couple, she picked up their exchange.

"He was smiling and I heard him say, "Calm down, baby. I love you."

McFall said she didn't know the woman who was screaming incoherently. And there was something evident about her hair.

"There was a strong breeze blowing. Her hair was blowing in the wind. It did not appear to be wet," said McFall.

She said neither Maurice nor Amanda ever came to the ambulance to check on the children.

McFall testified how Christopher's death, despite every best medical and rescue effort, was a blow to her gut, and that she needed a few minutes to decompress outside the confines of the emergency room.

Ten feet away from the picnic table where McFall and several other emergency responders sat, McFall testified, was Amanda Hamm, smoking a cigarette and taking her own break from the stressful situation.

"What I saw was that she was showing very little emotion. She was not crying. She was not upset until a family member or a friend came out and paid attention," said McFall in an opinion that drew a strong objection from Justice. An agreement had been reached that witnesses were not allowed to offer opinions, yet McFall had managed to interject some of the most negatives personal views to be offered by a witness.

Judge Peters allowed McFall's answer to stand based on the fact that both sides had used the term "hysterical" in their questions.

Later, after Kyleigh was on her way to Peoria on a medical flight, McFall said she saw Maurice standing nearby. "He was very calm, didn't seem upset at all," she observed.

The distressing experience of the accident, finding and dragging the children from the car, only to lose them, took a lasting toll on McFall and Over. Both left their jobs with the ambulance company and became security officers at the nuclear power plant on the shore of Clinton Lake.

Chapter Twenty-five

The state's heavy hammer dropped once again with testimony from the doctors and others who had worked for more than an hour to save the children. They were part of the state's strategy to immerse jurors in how Amanda and Maurice reacted to the lake incident.

The challenge was that Judge Peters had ruled witnesses could tell what they saw but offer no opinions about it.

Dr. Brit Williams, the physician who treated Christopher, was of minimal help to the state's endeavor. He said he wanted to ask Amanda some questions about what had happened to her son, but she was too upset to respond. Williams didn't speak to Maurice.

Dr. David Gill provided more fuel for the state's fire with what he remembered about Maurice. The doctor couldn't recall anything about Maurice's clothing but he had not forgotten his demeanor.

"There was a calmness. He didn't have the distraught manner that Miss Hamm had," Gill testified.

Under cross examination, Justice reminded Gill of statements he had given about Amanda in a deposition. When she learned that her son wouldn't make it, she was clearly distressed, the doctor confirmed.

The lawyers and judge had a short discussion before prosecutors called Dr. Tricia Scerba to the stand. Justice was especially concerned she would be quick to render an opinion about Amanda's behavior and comments when she visited her dead sons in the emergency room.

Amanda's state of mind had no place in Maurice's trial, Justice argued.

Prosecutor Ed Parkinson's objection was blunt.

"Well that's a brand-new argument he just offers. We never heard that one before," said Parkinson. He reminded the judge of his previous ruling that the deaths may have been the result of a conspiracy, a decision that likely impacted how the case would move forward, clearing the way for the state to use evidence that otherwise might be excluded, such as hearsay statements and opinions on how Maurice and Amanda were perceived by neighbors, teachers and relatives.

The judge asked Parkinson how the doctor's view of Amanda's apology to her dead child was relevant in Maurice's trial.

"Well, it's all part of the package of how Amanda behaved at the hospital," he answered. "I think it's relevant to her whole state of mind and how it fit in with the actions that they participated in together at the boat ramp."

The judge sided with the defense and barred the doctor from repeating the "I'm sorry" remarks Amanda made to her children.

Once on the stand, Dr. Scerba recounted efforts to resuscitate Kyleigh, medical procedures that produced that brief glimmer of hope the girl could survive. The doctor also described the two interactions she had with the infant's mother at the hospital. The two first met around 9 p.m. after Kyleigh's heart rate stabilized.

Scerba found Amanda, with Maurice sitting next to her, in the hospital chapel, surrounded by family members, she said.

"They were sitting in pews in the room, and she was just sitting very quietly. And I believe they were crying but they were very quiet."

A few minutes later, Scerba testified, she and Dr. Gill went together to tell Amanda about the plan to move Kyleigh to Peoria. They also needed to tell her Christopher and Austin had died.

Scerba recalled how she offered to take Amanda to Kyleigh so she could see her daughter before the helicopter arrived.

The doctor said she extended her arm around Amanda's shoulder to steady the tall woman. As the two walked down the hall to the treatment room, Scerba noticed Amanda's hair.

"It was longer, past her shoulders, and it was dry," she said.

Ruth Ann Staton, known as Rani, had worked at the Clinton hospital almost 30 years when she was called to provide nursing services for Austin that night. From the moment she sat in the witness chair, it was clear her testimony would stretch the bounds of the judge's ruling on what witnesses could observe about the mother's reaction.

"She seemed somewhat detached," Staton said of Amanda's visit with Austin as he lay dead in the ER. Amanda remained in the room "two or three minutes, tops" and may not have even touched the boy, said the nurse. The same tone and detachment applied to Amanda's visit with Christopher, Staton testified.

The area of inquiry was clearly touching a nerve with Justice. He objected multiple times. When the questioning shifted to what Amanda may have said about future plans, the judge sent the jury out while the matter was aired.

Anything the nurse heard from Amanda should be excluded, argued Justice, because it was hearsay and inadmissible even under the state's conspiracy theory.

Simpson tried to make a case for what Staton had to offer the jury: As Amanda sat in the hallway, steps away from her dead sons and a daughter barely clinging to life, she told the nurse she and Maurice had planned a move to St. Louis. And Amanda wondered out loud if events of the past several hours would change those plans.

"Do we think this evidence shows a guilty state of mind? Absolutely," argued Simpson.

The judge ruled Amanda's statement could be considered an act that supported the alleged conspiracy. Justice and Simpson agreed it would be best to ask Staton some questions before the jury returned to see where her testimony might lead and deal with any legal kinks outside earshot of jurors.

Staton couldn't say for sure whether Amanda's comment about the move to St. Louis came before or after she gave Amanda an injection of the tranquilizer Ativan. She was sure Amanda was lying on a gurney when the conversation took place.

Staton's response to a question about why Amanda was given medication showed how the first layer of skepticism about the drownings began to form.

"At that point, we were trying to give her the benefit of the doubt," said Staton.

With the practice session over, Staton repeated for jurors Amanda's statement about plans to go to St. Louis.

Linda Stickney, the nurse paired with Dr. Scerba to care for Kyleigh, saw Amanda visit her daughter before the medical flight.

"She stood close to the cot that Kyleigh was on. I don't remember her touching the child."

Again, the tone of Amanda's voice was an issue. And again, her words were described as "detached."

The jury got the day off on March 16 as the lawyers and judge returned to Clinton for a hearing on which of Amanda's statements the jury should hear. Simpson's copy of the statements measured three inches thick. Prosecutors were intent on extending their momentum by laying as much negative evidence as possible in front of jurors.

This time the evidence centered on what three people—one of them a woman who considered herself Amanda's best friend since third grade—told police about their conversations with Amanda shortly after the drownings.

Peters ruled statements normally judged as hearsay could be used by the state because they could reflect Amanda's purported efforts to conceal what the state characterized as murder.

At the same hearing, Simpson criticized Justice for handing documents to reporters sitting in the first row behind the defense table. Parkinson chimed in. He called Justice "Mr. Publicity."

Chapter Twenty-six

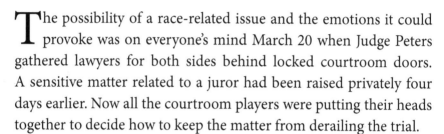

The possibility of a race-related issue and the emotions it could provoke was on everyone's mind March 20 when Judge Peters gathered lawyers for both sides behind locked courtroom doors. A sensitive matter related to a juror had been raised privately four days earlier. Now all the courtroom players were putting their heads together to decide how to keep the matter from derailing the trial.

A DeWitt County jail inmate had relayed information to a jailer about a conversation he'd had with an alternate juror, an acquaintance, who wanted to know if a man on the witness list was someone she had known in grade school. The inmate also quoted the woman, who was black, as saying she would not convict a black man.

Outside the courtroom, reporters were becoming vocal about being excluded without explanation. Inside, Judge Peters wondered out loud how to explain the inquiry to the media.

"I know they will be pounding on the door—someone's door— whether yours or Mr. Justice's," the judge told Simpson.

The woman, one of two blacks on the panel, was allowed to stay on the jury and told to stop talking to people about the trial.

A snowstorm kept the courthouse closed on March 21. When the trial resumed the next day, Judge Peters told those in the courtroom the closed hearing involved an unspecified jury issue. He provided no other details. When jurors were brought in, they were again cautioned not to discuss the proceedings with anyone.

Dressed in his crisply-pressed uniform, Sergeant Duane Pitchford, a district supervisor for the Illinois Department of Natural Resources, could have been mistaken for a military officer as he stepped forward, raising his right hand to take the oath to tell the truth.

He said he was at his home near Farmer City, some 20 miles from the west access boat ramp, when he got the call about the incident. By the time he arrived at 8:15 p.m., the commotion surrounding the rescue had ended.

Pitchford secured the scene and arranged for a dive team to drag the car from the water an hour later.

When he arrived at the hospital at about midnight, Pitchford and fellow conservation officer Doug Heusner were asked by the sheriff to keep an eye on Maurice.

"We were both asked to observe him because of concern for conflict between family members and Mr. LaGrone. It was highly emotional at the time," Pitchford testified.

But Maurice seemed to be outside the zone of high emotion.

"I couldn't determine any emotional response or reaction from him. He was very emotionless," the officer said.

With a photograph displayed on a large courtroom screen, the physical features of a boat ramp were explained to the jury. Pitchford said the west side ramp was among several Clinton Lake ramps resurfaced three years before the drownings to keep vehicles from sliding into the water as boats were launched or removed on the slippery surface.

If jurors couldn't get a clear understanding of the ramp texture from the photo, the heavy chunk of pavement wheeled into the courtroom on a cart would help. Pitchford stepped down from the witness stand to examine the sample and testify to the reason for the heavily grooved surface.

Since the ramps were renovated several years before the drownings, five vehicles had gone into the lake, he said. The single incident where a vehicle went into the water from a front-facing position occurred when a stolen pick-up truck was ditched in the lake and discovered two years later.

Sometimes there were mechanical problems, Pitchford said, but human error was usually why vehicles wound up in the water, both before and after the ramps were coated with the new rough surface. But the situation that resulted in three children's deaths was a first for Pitchford.

"I never seen anything like this, an occupied vehicle going into the water head-in," he said.

Under cross examination, Pitchford admitted he became "very curious" about the circumstances soon after he realized no boat was involved. And he passed his suspicions along to the sheriff in a phone call before 9 o'clock that night, adding to the growing awareness by law enforcement that it may not have been an accident.

As the trial continued, courtroom spectators divided like guests in a wedding chapel, sitting behind the person they supported. The long hallway outside the courtroom provided ample space for relatives and friends on the opposing sides to avoid each other.

Things got personal when people who had known Amanda and her family since childhood were called to testify. Beverly Clymer told jurors she considered herself Amanda's best friend. The two of them shared some common life experiences: Both knew what it was like to try to make ends meet as single mothers of young children from multiple fathers. The day before the lake incident, Clymer used three dollars she had borrowed from Amanda to put gas in her car to get to a job interview. She was at home with her boyfriend and four children in Hallsville, a village just west of Clinton, when her older sister called with news that a car had gone into the lake with three children inside. Clymer was worried Amanda's family might be involved.

"I started getting a bad feeling after the phone call," she said. "I just thought something bad was going to happen." She offered no basis for her fear.

When it was confirmed that her best friend's children were involved, Clymer said she was willing to join the rescue efforts.

"I was ready to go get in the lake myself and get them. I mean, they were my heart, too," she said.

At the back of the courtroom, Amanda's mother was having a hard time controlling her emotions. Beverly and Amanda had been close friends forever. Around 10 o'clock that night, Clymer testified, she met her younger sister and a friend at the hospital. Clymer spotted Amanda in the hallway.

"She was sitting in the wheelchair, and she had her head down. And then she looked up at me. She told me that the kids were gone."

Clymer said she demanded answers from Amanda.

"I said, 'What do you mean they are gone?' She said they had died. I didn't know what to say, what to do. You know, I was upset. It hurt, and it was just sad to see. I mean, there was no tears coming from her eyes," said Clymer, adding an unsolicited observation.

One of her first questions to Amanda made it clear she was no fan of Maurice. "Did Maurice do this?" she asked.

Amanda became irate, countering to her friend, "You're accusing him just because he's black," Clymer acknowledged in questioning from Tom Griffith.

Amanda's story about the incident changed three times, Clymer said.

First, Amanda said the trip to the lake was a way to waste some time before taking the children to a movie. The car was in reverse when Maurice hit the gas and the car lurched forward into the water.

In the second account, everyone fell asleep as the car was parked on the ramp and Maurice's foot slipped off the brake, sending the car rolling down the ramp into the water.

Finally, Clymer recalled an explanation that had everyone in the car "and instead of putting the car in reverse, he put it in drive, and they went forward and went into the water."

From the viewpoint of the defense teams in both murder cases, the last version was the most reasonable explanation.

Maurice had given Clymer reasons to dislike him. She told jurors about the day before the drownings when she stopped by Amanda's apartment to tell her about a lead for a possible job and was met by Maurice, sitting on the couch, in boxer shorts.

He touched her dress and propositioned her, she said—something she rejected because both were romantically involved with other people. She didn't tell Amanda about the encounter.

During the two decades they had known each other, Amanda and Clymer had seen the best and worst of each other's lives. But it was the darker moments of Amanda's life that the state wanted Clymer to highlight for the jury, starting with why Amanda became pregnant with Kyleigh.

At a sidebar meeting with the judge, Justice contended Clymer's anticipated testimony that Amanda had plans to trap Shane Senters into marriage amounted to character assassination.

"Amanda's personality, who she is and her life before this incident is not relevant in this case," Justice argued. "This is nothing more than saying she is a slut, and therefore she must have murdered her children."

Still in the lawyers' huddle, Simpson countered the state intended only to show how Amanda's life revolved around a desperate search for a husband and Maurice became that hope after the fathers of her three children walked away. "She is so thrilled, adamant and enamored with the relationship that, despite the fact he is abusive, she will stay with him. She will stay with him even though he is domineering and manipulative, even though he is self-indulgent," Simpson continued.

Prosecutor Parkinson further clarified the state's position. The negative inferences from Clymer's testimony would help the jury understand why Amanda's longing for a husband developed into a plot to kill her children.

Clymer would paint a picture of "a progression where a mother would get into a situation where she would allow her live-in boyfriend to take such drastic measures," Parkinson argued. "She chose. This is the one witness who can assist the jury in explaining a rather extraordinary set of progressions."

The judge allowed the state to ask its questions but cautioned prosecutors they would not be allowed to stray into character assassination. Nevertheless, when questioning resumed, the state had wide latitude on the areas of Amanda's life it could explore.

There were noticeable changes in Amanda after she met Maurice, according to Clymer.

"She changed by her appearance. The way she talked. The way she acted. Things she would do. Even her attitude towards her children had changed," said Clymer. And Amanda was rude to Clymer's children and came to visit less often. Sometimes Amanda asked to borrow money for groceries from the woman whose financial straits mirrored her own, she said.

Mixed perceptions about Amanda's household persisted as Clymer closed her testimony. She couldn't recall ever seeing Maurice do anything inappropriate to the children, and she did remember Amanda being in a good mood when Clymer stopped by Grecian Gardens to visit her at work just hours before the fatal trip to Clinton Lake.

Chapter Twenty-seven

It was like a bowl of milk for hungry kittens. Jurors appeared to lap up the array of questions and doubts Amanda's relatives raised with her and Maurice after little Kyleigh died.

Amanda's cousin, Jackie Polen, remained a harsh critic of the affectionate exchanges between Amanda and her boyfriend as Kyleigh slipped closer to death in the Peoria hospital.

"They were being inappropriate, kissing and hugging. They weren't consoling," Polen testified.

Polen took a moment to compose herself as she recounted her niece's death process, organs shutting down and life support withdrawn when the inevitable could no longer be ignored.

Jeff Justice got right to the point. "Fair statement: You really don't like Maurice very much, do you? In fact, you think he is guilty as hell, don't you?" he demanded.

Polen admitted her dislike for Maurice, but the judge would not let her give her opinion on Maurice's guilt.

She recalled a confrontation between Amanda and Austin's father, Craig Brown, at the hospital. Brown accused Maurice of being responsible for the car going into the water.

"It was that fucking nigger that killed my child," Polen quoted Brown as saying. Amanda came to her boyfriend's defense, denying Maurice had done anything to harm the children, she said.

Next to testify was Kathy Clifton, Polen's mother and Ann Danison's sister. She was so anxious that she asked that her daughter be allowed to remain in the courtroom for support during her testimony. Simpson supported the request, even though there was a general rule against witnesses being permitted in the courtroom. "I want to tell you all this woman is a wreck," the prosecutor offered while Clifton waited outside. "You thought the other girls were nervous—she is breaking new records."

Indeed, the experience of being in front of the jury, talking about the tragedy that had split the family, rattled Clifton. She offered short, concise answers in an uneven voice that betrayed her anxiety.

In describing the chaos at her sister's home where family gathered after Kyleigh's death, Kathy said Maurice's demeanor added to the tension.

"Pardon me, but he was really jive-talking about all of this. And it was really frustrating," Clifton said, explaining that "one thing led to another" and the cops were summoned to the house to remove Maurice.

The family learned from Amanda that night that Maurice had refused to follow her directions on how to safely back the car up the ramp. Clifton remembered Amanda telling relatives that while tragically wrong, Maurice did not intend to drive into the lake. But in the midst of crushing grief, Amanda's family was incapable of processing the possible difference between an intent to harm the children and sheer incompetence, she recalled.

Credibility is usually earned after a person passes a litmus test for truthfulness. Jurors were faced with making just such a determination as they took in the testimony of two federal inmates housed with Maurice during his long stay in the DeWitt County jail.

Jerry Peters, a 39-year-old released from federal custody in 2005, was a convicted counterfeiter with a criminal history dating back to his teenage years. Peters said Maurice got angry when he asked him why he didn't do more to save the children.

"The kids don't mean nothing to him anyway,' is the remark he made," Peters testified. "And that kind of upset me and I seen a different side of him I didn't see before."

Aside from a claim that Maurice bragged about his ability to control "hoes," a term for white, promiscuous women, Peters offered no confessions from Maurice—not even an admission that Maurice harmed the children.

During a morning break, Detective Rick Hawn could hardly contain his excitement about the next witness. Jailhouse informant Dwight Hayden had become acquainted with Maurice at the DeWitt County facility. His testimony promised to be hair-raising, even shocking, Hawn promised reporters.

Hayden was 54, with a lifelong criminal history. It was a federal conviction for passing fake checks that temporarily landed him in the DeWitt County jail. He and Maurice were housed in the same area between March and May of 2004.

Hayden's account of what Maurice told him about the drownings had surfaced during detectives' survey of inmates housed with Maurice.

Detectives Hawn and Panizo found Hayden later in Chicago's Metropolitan Correctional Center. He refused to talk with them. As they left, Hawn urged the inmate "to think about the children."

About a month later, Hayden wrote police, saying he had valuable information. Within days, Hawn and Panizo were back in Chicago, ready to record Hayden's statement.

Now, on the stand, Hayden testified how his deceased mother appeared to him in a dream, urging him to step forward.

"Me and her was real close," he told jurors. "My mom was into childcare and she was trying to tell me to do the right thing in my dream. She had three little children on her lap and they were crying.

They were asking her to ask me to let the court know what LaGrone had told me."

Hayden's recollection of the paranormal experience had the full attention of everyone in the courtroom—most of all jurors. Some looked skeptical.

Hayden said Maurice seemed to regard him as a mentor, that they read scripture together and talked about women. He at first believed Maurice was innocent. But then, during one encounter, Hayden said Maurice told him, "Man, I killed those kids."

"He said he told his girlfriend to shut up, that it was a done deal," Hayden testified, that when Maurice described the car sinking into the lake "he had a smirk on his face."

Under cross-examination, Hayden admitted his involvement in Maurice's case may have been influenced by more than his mother's appearance in a dream. He had also heard talk around the DeWitt County cell block about opportunities the murder case could offer a willing snitch.

Justice produced a letter Hayden had written federal prosecutors, demanding that in return for his testimony about Maurice, Hayden's friend be given a reduced sentence.

"I will take a lie detector test. Go before a grand jury. Video my statement but I must have overwhelming assurance that everything I have done so far as (sic) and willing to do is solely credited to my friend Terry Thomas," Hayden wrote, referring to the close friend facing a stiff federal sentence at the time.

The defense attorney also had jurors listen to about half of a three-hour recording of Hayden's interview with Hawn and Panizo. They heard Hayden say Maurice's uncle had urged Maurice to sell the children or kill them for insurance money, that the same uncle served as a getaway driver from the lake after the drownings. They also heard Hayden say Maurice had claimed he met Amanda through a cocaine dealer and that the couple had planned to kill the children a week earlier but didn't because the lake was busy with visitors.

Hayden had no answer when Justice quizzed him about why those statements weren't part of his current courtroom testimony. But Hayden did admit that just months before he volunteered information to police, he had told a defense investigator that he never heard Maurice talk about the children's death.

Justice also asked why Hayden only recently had told authorities about the dream sequence.

"I told Detective Hawn about my dreams the other night because I didn't know if anybody would understand," he answered.

For Hayden, the dream "was the decisive moment that I knew I had to come forth with the truth."

Jailhouse informants had given jurors a lot to think about, starting with how to separate fiction from truth.

Chapter Twenty-eight

Detective Hawn was precise in his testimony. His observations about the ramp, Christopher's lost baseball cap and the condition of the car were lasers aimed to dissolve any juror's thought that this was just a tragic accident involving two incompetent adults.

On the ramp: It was not slick. No algae covered the surface. There were no skid marks.

The baseball cap floated out of the car when Hawn opened the rear passenger door and it drifted towards a cove south of the boat ramp—an account that differed from Amanda's claim that the hat floated away before she and Maurice had loaded the kids into the car. Hawn said he saw no immediate reason to pick up the hat, toys, diapers and sippy cups collected the next day by another officer.

His statements on the car: Its doors opened freely. The passenger side window was almost completely down. Amanda's water-soaked purse was among things found inside.

Issues involving the submerged car's door locks were the focus of Tom Griffith's questions to Tom Lane, the local mechanic asked by police to get the car running again two days after it was pulled from the water.

Lane said the locks were unpredictable, that they'd suddenly operate on their own.

"Without any consistency, the doors would lock and unlock, or the door locks would actually quiver in the down position or lock position or in the unlock position," he explained.

On Sept. 6, with the car back on the boat ramp, ready for the re-enactment, he said the doors suddenly locked again with no prompting from anyone.

Sheriff Massey, one of the few witnesses allowed to remain in the courtroom during the testimony of others, had only a short walk from his seat when it was his turn on the witness stand. He testified he knew as soon as he arrived at the lake that "it was a significant incident," based on the unusual circumstances and the number of victims pulled from the water.

The sheriff said he decided he should be the one to interview Maurice and that another officer should speak to Amanda, she being the daughter of Ann Danison, a county employee Massey dealt with on a regular basis. The sheriff was never asked, nor did he explain how he set that opinion aside to become involved in more than a half dozen additional interviews with Amanda in the following days.

In Maurice, he said, he saw a calm individual, devoid of emotion. Massey said he told Maurice during their first interview at the hospital that the public would be curious about the incident.

"I said, 'Maurice, there are going to be a lot of people asking some tough questions, and one of those will be why you did not go back into the water to get the kids out of the car or rescue the kids,'" the sheriff recalled for the jury.

Maurice's reply, Massey said, was "I did everything I could for those kids."

As jurors watched video of seven tests performed on Sept. 6, 2003 using Amanda's car, Massey explained they were done to determine whether the car would respond in the way Maurice had described to police.

In his department's tests, the sheriff said the car's brakes functioned properly and the vehicle made it up the ramp after it was shifted into reverse. The tires, he said, did not spin.

Massey acknowledged attempts to recreate Maurice's version of events stopped short of all the details. "We did not do any tests with an occupant that tried to leave the vehicle," said the sheriff.

With the jury excused for the weekend, Parkinson rekindled a prosecution request. It had been a year since Judge Peters turned down the suggestion that jurors should visit the lake.

Just a 35-minute bus ride could enhance jurors' understanding of the scene beyond the ability of photographs, Parkinson argued. And the process would be fast and simple.

"They get out. No questions are asked. Deputies are there. They look around. They get back on the bus and we come back," he said.

Parkinson suggested the judge could even ask jurors whether a visit would be helpful, ideally before the state closed its case in just a few days.

Predictably, the defense was steadfast in its opposition to a road trip. Justice had a sarcastic suggestion of his own: How about a live reenactment with defense expert Michael Varat behind the wheel?

"If we are going to go to the scene, I would like to have Mr. Varat bring his car out and we'll run it in the water and have a driver get out," said Justice, clearly irritated with the state's resuscitation of the issue. "If we are going to reconstruct this thing, let's reconstruct the whole thing."

Peters again denied the state's request, saying a lot of things could happen during a visit to the lake "and about 99 percent of them are bad. We are not going to introduce that into this case."

On April 11, after two weeks of testimony from 37 witnesses, the state called its final witness, Amanda Hamm.

It was widely anticipated she would refuse to testify, instead asserting her constitutional right against self-incrimination. But her attorney, Steve Skelton, left the decision up to her.

Maurice's co-defendant entered the quiet courtroom wearing a baggy, ill-fitting long dress bought for her by her mother. The dress masked the pounds Amanda had gained since she went to jail. Almost immediately she became emotional as she looked down at the array of photos of her children spread out among other exhibits at the front of the courtroom. The jury hadn't been brought in yet.

Her legal team of Skelton, D. Peter Wise and John Hanlon stood with her as Parkinson asked that Amanda take the witness stand to answer some basic questions to determine her level of cooperation.

"Were you at the boat ramp?" Parkinson asked.

"I assert my Fifth Amendment privilege against self-incrimination," Amanda responded in a tone so soft it required people to lean forward to catch the phrase she had rehearsed over and over before coming into the courtroom.

Despite the state's offer of "use immunity" that would protect her from having her statements used against her at her own trial, Amanda refused to answer Parkinson's questions.

She left the courtroom without providing any testimony for the state and without looking directly at her former boyfriend.

The jury was unaware that Amanda had been in the courtroom. The contempt of court finding by the judge against Amanda for refusing his order to testify was never pursued by the state.

As is routine in many criminal cases at the close of the prosecution's case, the defense asked for a directed verdict, arguing the state had failed to meet its burden of proof beyond a reasonable doubt.

The inconsistency of witness statements alone raised reasonable doubt that the children's deaths were intentional, Justice argued, suggesting some witnesses had a motive for their damning recollections.

"I think we have a situation where their opinion of the case gets in the way of their memory," he said.

He argued testimony from a federal inmate, Hayden—the only evidence that Maurice committed a crime–was tainted by the favor he wanted for a friend and wrapped in the bizarre cloak of a dream. "I can't imagine any fact finder would consider the statement of Mr. Hayden reliable in any way, shape or form," Justice concluded.

It's up to the jury to determine the credibility of all the witnesses, Simpson countered, including the varying accounts by Amanda in her police interviews. Her words, he said, should be weighed by the jury in the context of testimony from other witnesses.

The prosecutor stepped closer to the empty jury box. His words, delivered slowly and with the seriousness of the life and death decision he wanted jurors to make, left no room for doubt that only they could deliver justice for Amanda's children.

"If there ever was a case that cries out for trial by jury, this is it," he said.

Peters denied the motion for a directed verdict, a request that if granted would have ended the trial in Maurice's favor. The assessment of the credibility of prosecution witnesses and the over-all strength of the state's case would be left to the jury. But not until the defense presented its case.

Chapter Twenty-nine

Maurice knew stakes were high when he raised his right hand and swore to tell the truth. He was the first witness in his own defense.

Speaking in a voice so soft that his attorney asked him to speak up, Maurice answered questions about his childhood, about things he would rather forget, including the death of his mother and a sequence of living with relatives, a cycle that lasted until he was jailed on murder charges.

Reliving the history brought Maurice to tears.

The jury learned about his string of low wage jobs, about the long parade of girlfriends—all of them mothers of young children. Photos of Maurice with the women and his two sons—the one who had died and a second produced during another relationship—were passed among the jurors. They spent just a moment looking at the images and then handed them down the row.

A large display of photos of places Maurice had lived in his 27 years of freedom contained 23 different images. The last of them showed the apartment he shared with Amanda and the children.

Maurice concurred with his attorney's assessment that Amanda was his fourth serious girlfriend.

Just two weeks after they met at the factory job in Heyworth, Maurice said, there was a mutual decision that he should move into her apartment in Clinton. She had been driving him to and from Bloomington.

Two or three months after that, there were problems.

"Financial problems. Fidelity problems because I guess by that time, I didn't really find her attractive in that way anymore. So, we had problems with sex," Maurice testified. "Sometimes I didn't want to have sex and we'd argue about things like that." He said when Amanda found he had phone numbers of other women, she was understandably jealous. "She had no problems with letting me know."

At times, disagreements turned physical.

During one fight, things got heated, Maurice said. "I slapped her."

Jurors seemed to pay full attention to Maurice's every word.

A second dispute erupted over cocaine Amanda bought with part of her income tax refund.

"I had been through a lot as far as people using cocaine," Maurice told the jury. "I didn't want that to happen between her and me." Another time, he said, he choked Amanda during a disagreement. But, he said, it was "nothing too serious."

Maurice stayed in Clinton despite his diminished feelings for Amanda.

"I had love for her. I wasn't in love with her," he said.

There was an emotional attachment to the kids, too, Maurice said. "Aside from that, I didn't have anywhere else to go."

Maurice wasn't totally committed to Amanda's dream of relocating to St. Louis for college and a better future. But he was willing to tag along because he'd be close to his family, plus his work towards a GED in Clinton would set him up for more education in St. Louis, he said.

Tom Griffith drilled into Maurice's interaction with children—a maneuver his lawyer hoped would counter some of the headway the state had made with its witnesses.

The questions started with how Maurice played with young relatives.

There was rough-housing with the boys and with the girls, Maurice said—games that sometimes scared his cousins.

Playtime with Amanda's children wasn't all that different. He'd shoot hoops or play catch with Christopher while Austin rode his tricycle around the playground.

Maurice paralleled his attachment to Kyleigh with his infrequent contact with his own son, who lived in St. Louis. "My son wasn't really in my life at the time. Her father wasn't really in her life at the time. We both had an absence, and we took to each other."

A series of photos showing Maurice and Amanda doing things with the kids was displayed on the courtroom screen. They reflected happiness, children building a snowman, picnicking in a park.

Weldon Springs State Park south of Clinton was the family's favorite spot for picnics and letting the youngsters burn off energy. A popular place for camping and hiking, the park also had row boats for rent.

A boat ride at Weldon Springs was something Amanda's sons often asked about but never something the two adults and three children managed to do, said Maurice.

"It was a task to get them to sit down and eat after they seen the boats" during the outings to Weldon Springs, Maurice recalled.

Griffith moved on to the pranks Maurice played with the children, starting with the incident involving Austin and the oven.

"We was playing around with the kids. I thought I'd have a little fun with them. So I picked them up and went over to the oven and acted as if I was going to stuff them in the oven. The oven hadn't been on for hours. It was cold. I acted as if I was turning the key, but I hadn't. And that was it. It was a joke."

Did Austin think it was funny? Griffith asked.

"He probably didn't think it was that funny at all," said Maurice, shaking his head as if his poor judgment just now became clear to him.

Maurice also had to explain his bad judgment in interactions with women. Beverly Clymer's visit earlier the day of the drownings was the first example.

Yes, Maurice had flirted with her, had asked to touch her dress. But she had stepped closer to allow it, not once but twice, he said. Then she sat on the stairs and they continued to talk.

"Before she left, I told her that her man was a lucky man. She said so was Amanda, and she left 10 or 15 minutes later," said Maurice. The two agreed to keep their small encounter to themselves, never dreaming each would one day offer a different version of it while sitting in the witness stand at a murder trial.

Maurice was looking forward to relaxing later that night after dinner at The Shack, he said. With his sights on a couple rented movies and some marijuana, Maurice was unenthused over Amanda's spontaneous suggestion that they take the kids to Clinton Lake.

Despite his suspended driving privileges, he got behind the wheel and was entertaining the boys by speeding.

Now it was time for Maurice to explain why he parked on the boat ramp.

"I figured since vehicles park on boat ramps with boats attached to them, for one, I wouldn't have a problem backing up without a boat being attached to the vehicle," he said. "Aside from that, I ended up on the boat ramp because I was playing around with the kids, acting as if I was going to drive into the water, stopped a few feet before the water. And that's how I ended up on the boat ramp."

Maurice said Christopher thought the whole thing was funny, but his brother and mother were not amused.

Just how close the car was to the water became obvious as they left the car, Maurice said.

"Christopher and I had walked in front of the car. I remember it wasn't enough space for both of us to walk side-by-side."

After playtime was over, the two boys climbed into their seats and Kyleigh was strapped into her car seat that wasn't properly anchored to the car. Maurice recalled the apprehension he felt as he peered over the hood of the car and saw only water. Griffith asked Maurice if he recalled saying anything that reflected his anxiety.

"I said, 'It would be fucked up if the car went in the water.'" Maurice said he ignored Amanda's instruction to remove his foot from the brake slowly while she pushed on the accelerator with the car in reverse.

"I decided to do it my own way."

Jurors scribbled notes, trying to keep up with Maurice's lengthy narrative.

"Started the car, put the car in reverse, put my right arm behind Amanda's seat, told the kids to hold on. I was figuring I was going to go from the brake to the accelerator and there would be a jump going up in the ramp."

"Let me stop you there for a second," Griffith said. "Had Amanda been giving you some instructions?"

"Yes, she had."

"What did you say in response to that?"

"I told her, feeling insulted, I told her I could take care of it. I could do it. It would be no problem."

Maurice said he heard tires spinning as he shifted his foot from the brake to the accelerator. He thought the car was in reverse even though it moved forward into the lake.

"The car floated out a bit. During that time, I tried to roll down my window."

He said he hit a button for the automatic door locks before he turned towards Kyleigh in the back seat.

As the car began its nosedive into the water, panic set in.

"I hit the door about three times with my shoulder until the door finally came open. I proceeded to jump out of the car."

Maurice recalled his foot getting stuck as he was leaving and Amanda appearing out of nowhere on the driver's side of the car. She waded towards the shore to the pay phone to call for help, he said, and he started to follow before she turned and yelled to him, "Get my kids out of the car."

"I wasn't out of the water yet. I turned back around, went to the back door, pulled on the back door a few times. I didn't feel it catch, the door didn't open. I attempted to go through the window. I put my face in the water. That's as far as I was able to make it before panicking.

"I came back up, went back to the door again, pulled on it a few more times."

Panic turned to horror, Maurice said.

The witness looked intently at his lawyer, trying his best to compose rational answers for a jury he hoped would not judge too harshly his limited ability to communicate.

"At this time, I could see Austin standing in the back seat and I could see Christopher as well. Kyleigh was already underwater. I couldn't see her. I couldn't just stand there watching them go under the water like that, so I ran out of the water, up the boat ramp towards the pay phone. I could hear Amanda having difficulties on the phone, so I started talking to the operator, trying to give her directions where we were and how to get to the boat ramp."

Griffith interrupted Maurice's rambling account with more questions.

"Did you ever hit the brake as the car was going in the water?"

"No. I didn't.

"Why not?" Griffith asked.

"I panicked. I can't tell you why. I didn't. I just didn't," answered Maurice.

As emergency crews arrived and accomplished what Amanda and Maurice had failed to do, Maurice held his girlfriend back from the water.

"I didn't want her to go out there and hurt herself," he explained. "I didn't want her to see her children as they were bringing them out of the water. I did my best to keep her back from the situation, trying to console her so they could do their job effectively."

Griffith directed Maurice's attention to the search for answers to questions that began almost immediately after he and Amanda walked through the emergency room doors behind the rescuers carrying the children's limp bodies.

"Why did you continually talk with the police?" Griffith asked.

"So everyone would have an understanding as to what happened. I felt everybody deserved an explanation," Maurice responded.

As police drew in closer with their questions, Maurice searched for support, he said. He asked Sheriff Massey if he could use Massey's cell phone to call his family. Massey refused.

"I was distraught," said Maurice. "But at the same time, I didn't know where this thing was going, so I was confused. I became fearful in this situation, you know. I'm a black guy in Clinton. Don't nobody know what's going on. I was concerned."

In Peoria, the mood was equally somber as family hopes for Kyleigh faded. Maurice was in the room when the decision was made to discontinue life support.

"I sat on the window sill, just looking out the window, still disbelieving the whole situation. At one point I leaned over and kissed her on the cheek."

Griffith shifted to testimony from witnesses who judged the reactions of Maurice and Amanda the night of the tragedy.

Maurice said he and Amanda had walked into downtown Clinton to look for marijuana.

"I wanted to deal with grieving in my own way," he testified. "I wasn't concerned with anybody taking what I was doing as inconsiderate. But for me, smoking marijuana, being off to myself, was going to be my way of grieving. I didn't want to sit around and talk about nobody, so I proceeded to find some marijuana."

And yes, he acknowledged, he and Amanda had taken a shower together. It was an effort to save time, he said; they did not have sex in the bathroom. "That was it. Nothing more, nothing less."

Maurice told jurors accusations were thrown at him like darts when he and Amanda returned to Ann Powers' home from their Sept. 3 police interview.

As far as Maurice was concerned, he wasn't lying to Lindy Powers when he was asked about charges being filed after Maurice spoke to police on Sept. 2.

"It wasn't a charge in my mind since I was never really incarcerated or anything to that extreme. I'm thinking of charges—something I had done some time for, as opposed to a traffic ticket."

Fully aware the state possessed all of Maurice's statements, Griffith preemptively asked his witness about his truthfulness in the hours and days after the incident. Why, Griffith asked, did Maurice tell investigators he had applied the brakes before the car entered the water?

"I was responsible, and I felt responsible for what happened, and after the fact I felt like I could have done more. I knew I could have done more. I felt bad," Maurice continued. "So in an attempt to appear that I had done more than I had, I told them I applied the brakes."

There was a second lie about how close the car was parked to the water, a lie also told to varnish his lack of effort to protect the children, Maurice admitted.

"After the fact, I seen how foolish it was. Even though it was a mishap, I didn't want to appear as foolish, so I stated I parked further away than I did."

Maurice had more to worry about than being deemed foolish in the hours after Kyleigh's death. Police considered him a child murderer and said as much during an interrogation, Maurice recalled. Those accusations, he said, were behind his remark to Amanda during the disagreement with family members.

"There was confusion in the house. I was concerned there was still chaos. I felt she could easily rectify that by explaining what happened. I said, 'we need to get our stories straight.'"

Neighbors in the apartment complex were starting to question Maurice's involvement in the deaths, too. He woke up Sept. 4 to a voice outside repeating the rumor that had spread overnight: "He's in jail."

"At this point I knew I was a suspect and being in Clinton at that time wasn't safe."

Maurice said he called his stepbrother in Bloomington to ask for a ride, and that while he waited, he picked up the kids' toys in the scrap of grass that passed for a front yard. The next time he came to Clinton, he'd be in a squad car, facing murder charges.

Griffith was ready to close his inquiry.

"Maurice, I ask you: On September 2, 2003, at approximately 7:41 p.m., did you intentionally drive that car into the water?"

"No, I didn't."

"Did you do it as some type of prank?"

"No, I didn't."

"How did you feel about those kids, Maurice?"

"I cared for those kids. I wasn't the best role model or father figure in their life but I cared about those kids," said Maurice, lowering his head in apparent embarrassment for his failure to be a better partner for Amanda and his inability to save her children.

"What are you going to have to live with the rest of your life?"

"Seeing Austin and Christopher standing up in the back of the window and Kyleigh already under the water. It was my last vision of them. I have to live with that as well as making a foolish mistake of parking on that ramp and panicking, getting out of the car like a coward, and not being able to do more than what I did. That's what I gotta deal with for the rest of my life."

Griffith paused, doing a final assessment of whether he had showed jurors how Maurice's unfortunate upbringing contributed to his self-centered lifestyle. When all the pieces of Maurice's broken life were assembled, Griffith hoped jurors found it hard to believe a man who lacked the ambition to be on time for work or the ability to make change at a gas station could concoct a plot to kill three children. And that the notion that he possessed a burning desire for a long and possessive relationship with Amanda—a woman he did not find attractive or love—was contrary to Maurice's history.

But had Maurice provided an explanation for his actions and inactions that jurors and the public could accept? Paralyzing panic, Griffith realized, might prove a hard sell.

Maurice sat, shaking his head in apparent disbelief at what had gone so wrong. The courtroom was silent. Maurice had been on the stand four hours.

Like a pitcher with his arm warmed up and eager to take the mound, Simpson wasted no time throwing fastballs at Maurice during the cross examination. Going straight to the issue of credibility, the prosecutor had no trouble getting Maurice to admit he had lied to police about how far the car was parked from the water's edge.

Simpson pursued explanations for other lies. Why had Maurice been untruthful about applying the brakes?

"Three children had died. You know, because I'm a black man in Clinton, it's a possibility I could be on trial for nine counts of murder," Maurice said in a defensive tone.

Concern instantly swept across the defense table. If it were raised at all, race was an issue that required great sensitivity. Having the defendant suggest his ethnicity was a reason for multiple lies could backfire.

The exchange became heated when Simpson asked Maurice about yet another lie he told concerning a fender bender that damaged Amanda's car. But that lie was different from the ones he told the sheriff, said Maurice, because he admitted his lies to Massey and "the fact that I got out of the car like a coward."

The pattern of lying mattered, Simpson told Maurice, because jurors would have to decide if he was being truthful about the single issue in the case: whether the children died in an accident or by way of an intentional act.

His voice heavy with sarcasm, Simpson asked Maurice to tell jurors when he stopped lying to police.

The truth came out on "small details," said Maurice.

"It was a situation that went out of control. I did the best I could have done. I could have done more. I don't feel it was a major issue to where my life should be put on the line," said Maurice, still trying to explain the untruths.

Maurice's character took more hits with his matter-of-fact answers to Simpson's questions about his womanizing, even while with Amanda.

"When did you start looking for other women to satisfy?" Simpson asked.

"Probably there wasn't a moment I wasn't looking for a woman to satisfy me. I wasn't faithful to her apparently," Maurice said with no noticeable regret.

Simpson wrapped up his three-hour cross examination with an observation wrapped in a question that made the point he wanted every juror to consider: By not hitting the brakes, Maurice had reacted differently than anyone else would, hadn't he?

Maurice conceded Simpson's point.

Chapter Thirty

Next up were witnesses who knew Maurice as a child and young adult. The effect, Tom Griffith hoped, would be a softening of his client's image, a perception that while Maurice may be flawed and never quite grew up, he was essentially a sincere person worthy of trust.

Tara Parker and Sandra Russell said they trusted Maurice with their children during the many hours he babysat for them. Maurice "had the patience of 10,000 men," Parker told jurors.

A practical step taken by Amanda towards her dream of moving to St. Louis with Maurice and the children was recalled by Shaunte Jefferson, Maurice's half-sister who managed a daycare in St. Louis. Childcare for Amanda's children was discussed during a July 2003 visit to the facility where Jefferson, who shared a mother in common with Maurice, supervised staff and youngsters left at the facility.

Ann Danison was blunt in what she saw in Maurice: a man she hoped would be only a temporary partner for her daughter for a variety of reasons, starting with his race.

"I wasn't crazy about the idea," she admitted. "I don't mean to bring race into it, but that had a lot to do with it. I was concerned about the kids." Small town thinking could have made things difficult for her grandchildren if their peers wanted to tease them about their mother's bi-racial romance, she said.

Amanda's mom was also displeased with Maurice's chronic failure to keep a job and his refusal to pitch in with childcare while her daughter worked multiple jobs to pay the bills.

Griffith asked Danison to describe Maurice's relationship with her grandchildren.

"They were close," she said.

She recalled watching Maurice and Christopher play basketball while Austin rode his tricycle nearby. He held and chased Kyleigh when she toddled away from her siblings. Danison testified she never witnessed any inappropriate conduct by Maurice with the children.

She said she asked the children deliberately subtle questions to determine whether everything was okay at home with Maurice. Never did they say anything to make Danison think her grandchildren feared him.

"If they did, I would have done something about it," she said. Likewise, she never saw bruises or signs of abuse on her daughter or grandkids.

The recitation of how the tragedy unfolded on Sept. 2 brought Danison to tears once again. She struggled through the memories of what she saw when she arrived at the hospital that night.

"We could see all these police cars and I knew it couldn't be my mom, so we ran in and there's Amanda and pretty much a big nightmare," recalled Danison.

She said the hours surrounding the deaths of her grandchildren were faint in her memory because tranquilizers had deadened much of the horror that took place in two hospitals. She was left with regret that her daughter had allowed a man to move in too soon.

In cross-examination, she was direct with Simpson. "Amanda never did pick the right man. She never did."

Danison could be forgiven if she thought it was her daughter, and not Maurice, who was on trial at the moment.

Next, the defense tried to address pesky questions over whether Maurice and Amanda's clothes were wet or dry.

Belinda Rittenhouse, a close friend of Danison and a hospital worker, was in a meeting there when she heard the chaos of multiple emergency vehicles arriving in the parking lot.

As a witness for the defense, she recalled how Amanda asked for some dry clothing to replace her soaking wet sweat pants and shirt. Maurice, she said, asked Rittenhouse to accompany Amanda into the locker room where she put on a pair of hospital scrubs.

When the two left the changing room, Rittenhouse gathered up the soggy clothes from a bench and put them in a bag, she said.

While at the hospital to support his daughter and check on the conditions of his three gravely injured grandchildren, Mark Walston watched the first interactions between Maurice and police.

One detail of a conversation he overheard between the sheriff and Maurice stuck out in his mind.

"Mr. Massey was asking him about the circumstances and what transpired," Walston said in response to a question from Justice, "and Maurice said he was trying to get out of the car, and the door slammed on his foot."

Prosecutor Parkinson's questions focused on how Walston became involved in Maurice's conversation with the sheriff. When Massey asked Maurice to move to a room so he could ask more questions, Walston asked to come along. When the sheriff began his inquiry, Walston stopped him. "Shouldn't you advise him of his rights?" Walston had asked.

Parkinson wanted to know why Walston, a gas company worker with no law enforcement experience, would ask such a question.

"What business was it of yours, if the sheriff was trying to find out what happened with three little kids found in the car? Why on earth would you suggest he advise Mr. LaGrone of his rights at that point?" Parkinson's tone was stern, hoping to convey that Walston had been out of line.

"I felt like it might be essential later," Walston answered. "I mean, I would have done the same thing if he was asking me questions about someone involved in a death."

The procession of witnesses willing to support aspects of the defense case grated on the nerves of Craig Brown, Austin's father. Outside the courtroom he complained about sympathetic testimony from Amanda's family, in particular what he viewed as Ann Danison's changed attitude.

"I believe she thinks if she helps Mr. LaGrone get off, she's going to help her daughter get out of it," said Brown.

Outside the courtroom, Danison responded she decided to stand by her daughter when more information became available as the investigation progressed, that it had nothing to do with saving Maurice from judgment.

"Emotions were running high," she told a reporter. "It was questionable at the beginning as to what happened. If I thought Maurice harmed my grandkids, I would want him to be punished for it. The evidence does not support guilt," she said.

Chapter Thirty-one

Dr. Mark Cunningham, a forensic psychologist whose experience included working with nuclear submarine crews, was called to explain how certain elements of human behavior were in play as Maurice and Amanda reacted to the drownings. Cunningham's friendly personality came through as he discussed how different people respond to emergency situations and how grief and stress accompany traumatic events.

The psychologist was an expert in his field. He gave long narrative answers and displayed charts to illustrate his points.

Roger Simpson lodged an ongoing objection to Cunningham's testimony about the psychological make-up of effective first responders. It was irrelevant, he said, because no one claimed Maurice was anything close to an emergency responder.

The judge disagreed with Simpson and let Cunningham explain why a positive childhood sets the tone for a career in saving lives. And why a dysfunctional upbringing could steer one away from such a job.

"Childhood is when the rebar goes into the concrete," said Cunningham. The sturdier the foundation a person has early in life, the better responder the person will be.

The untrained person has a variety of reactions to emergencies, the psychologist said.

People are heroes if they charge forward to save a life. Others are bystanders. Their actions, he said, can be further classified as culpable if their response is deemed ineffective, and culpable can move up a notch to malevolent if the ineffective response is tied to a definite plan or conspiracy.

To learn about Maurice, Cunningham spent seven hours with him and additional time with Ann Danison and Maurice's former girlfriends. The dysfunctional circumstances of Maurice's childhood had a lasting impact on his life, said the witness.

"The quality of Maurice's concrete is not going to be so good, even out of the chute" said Cunningham.

Justice tried to use Cunningham to purge the negative thoughts surrounding the shower Maurice and Amanda shared after Kyleigh's death.

Grief is personal, said the psychologist, and studies show that for one in three couples, the death of a child has no effect whatsoever on their sex life. A shower is one step removed from sex, he added.

Cunningham testified the trauma of losing three children could account for the various versions of events Amanda may have given to people at the hospital.

"This has been like a bomb going off in Amanda's head," Cunningham said of the trauma-related confusion she felt on Sept. 2. Christopher, Austin and Kyleigh defined Amanda as a mother and human being. The loss of that identity, combined with guilt for not saving them and her history of avoiding things that hurt her, all came crashing down around Amanda. It was little wonder she couldn't manage the situation effectively, said Cunningham.

Cunningham's easy-going style and ever-present smile didn't impress Simpson. To the contrary, the doctor's long dissertations seemed to rub Simpson the wrong way. When it came time for cross-examination, Simpson laid down the rules for Cunningham's responses—he wanted "yes or no, or I don't know."

Within a few minutes, however, Cunningham had returned to lengthy responses and Simpson tried repeatedly to turn off the spigot on what he considered a lecture.

By the time his cross-examination neared its end, Cunningham had unloaded a bag full of scientific explanations for the way Maurice and Amanda handled the aftermath of the lake incident. Still the state had done its best to get jurors to rely on good old common sense and consider Cunningham's testimony nothing more than psycho mumbo jumbo.

Even so, defense attorney Justice had more questions that turned Cunningham's focus to why he believed the murder of three children was so out of character for Maurice.

"Maurice's behavior response of choice is to walk away," Cunningham said. "This is a very dramatic departure for Maurice, not just because it represents a homicide—even greater than that: a triple homicide—but because it represents doing something really significant to address whatever's going on in his life. And that's not what Maurice has done up to this point."

Stepping down from the stand, Cunningham delivered another smile, believing he had effectively delivered his opinion.

Next to be heard was California automotive engineer Michael Varat about a series of tests performed on a car similar to Amanda's Oldsmobile. But the lawyers kept Judge Peters on the bench into the evening hours, arguing over which videos of the tests jurors should see. Most in dispute were tests performed at Lake Casitas, near Los Angeles, that included a stuntman's exit from the car as described by Maurice.

Simpson opposed elements of the tests that started on a 100-foot ramp, a significantly longer platform than the 30-foot boat entry at Clinton Lake.

The judge went home that night, re-thinking his ruling that barred video showing the stuntman's escape. When he returned to the courtroom for the trial's final day of testimony, the judge announced he had changed his mind. The jury would be allowed to see the video.

Varat provided commentary as jurors watched dramatic video of a car slowly tilting into the water and a man's movements to leave the submerged vehicle.

"If you exit while moving forward, there's water pressure against the door, about 140 pounds of pressure. Your foot is the last thing out, and when that diver escaped, the door came right back on his foot," said Varat, depicting a maneuver similar to what Maurice had described as he exited Amanda's car.

In cross-examination, Simpson called attention to disparities between the test and what had happened at the lake. The diver's journey into the lake was scripted, and a team of helpers was on the site.

Varat acknowledged he wasn't at Clinton Lake Sept. 2, so he couldn't say for certain that he was duplicating Maurice's action. But he said the California tests did replicate the car's position in the lake—26 feet from the water's edge—and gave jurors a visual understanding of a man's escape from a sinking car.

The defense brought back Detective Rick Hawn to clarify his experience with the unpredictable, almost spooky, door locks. As he walked around the car parked on the boat ramp just before the testing at Clinton Lake, Hawn noticed something. "We were locked out. I thought somebody played a joke on me," Hawn recalled.

On April 4, the defense closed its case with Maurice's uncle, a witness called to further deplete the credibility of testimony from the jailhouse informant. John LaGrone also reinforced the image of a family tree that produced Maurice growing straight and tall, despite weakness in some of its branches.

A retired school teacher from St. Louis, LaGrone was the brother of Maurice's father and had visited Maurice in jail about six weeks earlier. The uncle denied inmate Hayden's claim that he had advised Maurice to kill the children. Likewise, he said he made no offers to be the getaway driver after a murder.

Now, before closing arguments, Maurice and his defense team faced a major decision. They could ask the judge to give jurors the option of finding Maurice guilty of an offense less serious than murder.

After three conversations with his lawyers, Maurice rejected their recommended all-or-nothing approach. They finally agreed to request involuntary manslaughter as an alternative judgment.

But Judge Peters rejected the defense position that Maurice's conduct could be construed as reckless and therefore be considered involuntary manslaughter.

"It may approach negligence or something else, but I don't believe the lesser offense should be tendered to the jury," said the judge.

Ed Parkinson told reporters the ruling made sense. "This is pretty clear cut. It's either murder or an accident."

Griffith told the same reporters he was deeply concerned about one element as the case drew to a close.

"I don't believe the state has proven Maurice did this intentionally," the defense attorney said. "On the other hand, Maurice got up on the witness stand and said, 'It's my fault three kids are dead.'"

And jurors would not have involuntary manslaughter available as a point of compromise.

During his hours outside the courtroom, Griffith talked about the murder case with his father, a Decatur physician. The elder Griffith shared an opinion that likely mirrored the view of many people. At the end of the day, he told his son, three children are dead and it will be difficult to let someone go home after that.

Chapter Thirty-two

Roger Simpson was energized as he stepped in front of the jury box just after 9 a.m. He would present the state's closing argument.

It had been five weeks of long days for the prosecutor and the three other lawyers involved in the case. Jurors were also ready to bring the trial to an end.

Spectators filled every seat in the courtroom and included relatives of the defendants, of the children and of the lawyers. Silence muffled the room as Simpson reminded the jury the state was not required to prove, even provide, a motive for the drownings.

"How could there be a motive to kill three children whose cumulative ages don't even reach ten at the time of their deaths?" he asked.

Maurice's initial lies to police about how far he had parked from the lake's edge and whether he applied the brakes were not just a little fudging of the facts, said Simpson.

"They were whoppers, perhaps something he learned in the three weeks he worked at Burger King," the prosecutor sniped.

Maurice, seated at the defense table and in clear view of the jurors, shook his head in disagreement as the lead prosecutor painted a disapproving assessment of the evidence and of Maurice's immaturity and unwillingness to pull his weight in a relationship.

Simpson said jurors could dismiss testimony from automotive engineer Michael Varat because it was based on an assumption that Maurice was in the car when it went into the lake.

"There's not a shred of evidence that he was ever in that car," said Simpson.

In Simpson's view, the evidence and testimony, when considered as one body of work, pointed to guilt. If the LaGrone case were a movie, he said, its title would be "Proof Beyond a Reasonable Doubt."

After 90 minutes of review and evaluation of the testimony, Simpson closed his argument with a quote from Jimmy Stewart in the movie *Shenandoah*.

"If we don't try, we don't do. And if we don't do, then why are we here on this earth?" he said, referring to Maurice's lack of effort to save the children.

Jeff Justice was equally eager to take his post in front of the jury, to recite flaws the defense detected in the state's case.

A common thread stitched into the testimony of the state's very first witness and woven throughout the recollections of all the others, he said, was a dark and sinister inference assigned to Maurice and Amanda. Tears or no tears, wet or dry, the accused would never be given the benefit of the doubt.

The defense lawyer argued that after a tragic event, it's not uncommon for witnesses "to add a few things to make sure the outcome is what you want it to be." Such was the case with the people who served as caretakers for the children while their mother worked, at school and in the hospital as they fought for the children's lives, said Justice.

He challenged the state's theory that Maurice wasn't in the car as it was swept into the water.

"To say that Mr. LaGrone was never in that car is to ignore all the witnesses," said Justice, referring to those who saw Amanda's water-soaked clothes and relatives who gave their accounts of what Amanda and Maurice said about the accident.

He told jurors their decision about whether Maurice was guilty or innocent of murder should be based on fact, not emotion.

"Your job is not to provide justice for these children. You may feel he was careless, negligent and stupid for parking the car on a ramp. I won't disagree. But we're not here to measure the quality of his stupidness."

Justice returned to his seat, wondering whether he had said enough, whether he had said the right things.

Shortly after 2 p.m., the jury was escorted to a room down a secure hallway behind the fifth-floor courtroom to begin deliberations. More than 50 pieces of evidence, including the multiple large-scale drawings of the scene, were taken to the jury room.

Not long after that, jurors asked to hear the 911 tape. They listened to the four-minute tape about 20 times. Duct tape, markers and highlighters were also requested by the jury.

Ann Danison and other family members paced the hall outside the courtroom where reporters also gathered for the vigil.

"It's nerve-racking," Amanda's mother said. "I'm anxious for the verdict, but yet I'm scared."

The lawyers also waited. Friday afternoon threatened to become Friday night. Parkinson told reporters he wasn't surprised there was no quick verdict. "I'm sure it's going to take a while," he said. "There's a lot of evidence. This is a circumstantial case. But I think we've proven murder."

With no verdict reached by 6 p.m., jurors were sent home for the weekend. Lawyers had agreed jurors would not be sequestered during deliberations.

When they returned Monday, the jury asked to view the video of two automotive tests conducted by police. One showed how the car's brakes performed on the ramp. The other, conducted at the request of the defense, put the car into about a foot of water before it was backed up the ramp.

By late afternoon, jurors had a request for another video. It was of Maurice explaining his actions to police during their reenactment at the lake. It had been described by the defense in opening statements but never shown to jurors. Judge Peters denied the request. It was not part of the presented evidence.

The order and nature of the requests led lawyers for both sides to surmise the jury was reviewing the testimony of each witness in chronological order. Everyone settled in for a long wait. The lawyers returned to the courtroom when needed, but otherwise prosecutors waited in space provided by the McLean County state's attorney on the sixth floor, and the defense lawyers in Steve Skelton's office across the street.

As the jury worked behind closed doors, Maurice sat in his cell three floors below, awaiting the decision that would determine his fate. His lawyers said Maurice was "strong and putting forth a positive attitude."

Jurors ended Monday with no decision.

When they returned the next day, jurors wanted to examine some more evidence: four photographs of Maurice and the children, Dr. Cunningham's testimony on reactions to grief and emergencies, and a videotape of other tests involving the car. They received them.

At 4:30 p.m., the judge sent a message to jurors asking if they wanted to quit for the day. Word came back that they wanted to keep going. At 6 p.m., they had a question about how to sign the verdict forms. Thirty minutes after that, they informed the judge they had a verdict.

As they returned to the courtroom, jurors showed heavy wear and tear. They had deliberated 23 hours over three days. While the judge reviewed the verdict forms one-by-one, one male juror stared directly at Maurice, then put his hands over his eyes and looked at the floor.

Many in the audience struggled to contain their emotions—something the judge warned they must do or face ejection from the courtroom.

Maurice, with his lawyers on either side, stood to learn his fate.

Guilty, as to Austin Brown, of first-degree murder. Guilty as to Kyleigh Hamm. Guilty as to Christopher Hamm.

Maurice stood silent, showing no emotion. The spectators also stayed silent as those who were overjoyed with the decision kept their feelings under wraps for a few minutes more.

Jurors were directed to return the next day to decide if Maurice was eligible for the death penalty. If they agreed that he was, their next determination would be whether he should be executed, a decision that would come after a lengthy hearing with witnesses who had known Maurice since childhood.

Following a pre-arranged plan, police escorted jurors from the building. Ann Danison, sobbing and stunned, was shuffled away from a celebration that was about to erupt in the hallways and lobby of the courthouse.

Justice told reporters the defense team was "overwhelmingly shocked" by the verdicts. With the decision on the death penalty still looming, Justice said "We will stand strong tomorrow and next week. We're hoping we will be able to make sure Maurice leaves this courthouse with his life."

But for the fathers of the children and their families, the verdicts were confirmation of their belief the children died as a result of an intentional act. Family members who had waited hours for the decision hugged Parkinson and members of his prosecution team. When Justice met with Maurice a short time after the verdicts, Maurice said the verdict didn't surprise him.

"I knew they were gonna convict me," said Maurice, accepting the decision as another rung on his ladder that went nowhere.

After a 50-mile drive back to Decatur in a pouring rain, the defense lawyers mulled over arguments they would offer the jury the next day. Keenly aware their work was, in fact, a matter of life or death, Justice and Griffith both endured a restless night.

When court resumed the following morning with a convicted murderer now in the room, Griffith asked jurors to keep the term "knowingly" in mind. "He didn't do it intentionally or knowingly," Griffith said. Several jurors nodded, apparently in agreement. "But he parked a car three feet from the water, things got away from him, and the children ended up dying." That alone, Griffith suggested, should rule out a death penalty.

Simpson had a different view.

"While death was quiet—no one could hear it—it was brutal," he said.

It took jurors only ten minutes to decide Maurice was not eligible for a death sentence.

Judge Peters immediately sentenced Maurice to life in prison without the possibility of parole. Illinois law left the judge no other option in multiple murder convictions.

Stone faced, just as he was when the guilty verdicts were read, Maurice showed no emotion as the judge pronounced the life sentence. He was quickly taken from the courtroom, a move designed to provide him with privacy and keep the crowd from shouting what some were itching to say.

Several jurors agreed to speak with reporters. Surrounded by TV cameras and microphones in the lobby of the law and justice center, juror Greg Haddock said, "We didn't believe there was an intent, but he was put in a situation that got out of hand and didn't save them."

With at least one juror believing the deaths were not intentional, the verdict left a lingering question: Was Maurice found guilty of what he had done to the children or for what he had failed to do for them?

Shane Senters, father of Kyleigh Hamm, and Christopher's father, Greg Hamm, left the building with nothing to say to reporters, unwilling to reveal whether they were satisfied with a decision that spared Maurice LaGrone's life but meant he would spend the rest of it in prison.

The Coalition to Abolish the Death Penalty issued a statement critical of the state's decision to seek the death penalty in Maurice's trial and in the coming trial for Amanda, saying that because a capital case meant the state government would cover many of the prosecution expenses, the financial health of DeWitt County was put ahead of justice.

In his first public comment since the trial began, Simpson denied the death penalty request was based on money. Standing with the sheriff, Simpson said he accepted the jury's decision concerning the death penalty. "That's their call. I have no quarrel with that at all," he said.

Defense attorney Justice said the judge's refusal to give the jury a second option for a verdict would be solid grounds for an appeal. "I think the jury was left with no other choice. I'm convinced the jury was not going to let Maurice go home."

Back in his jail cell, Maurice removed his street clothes for the last time. His next stop was Joliet, a reception center for the Illinois Department of Corrections that would provide his home for the rest of his days.

Thirty miles away, in a DeWitt County jail cell, his former girlfriend awaited her day in court.

Chapter Thirty-three

The jury's decision to spare Maurice's life was small comfort for Ann Danison as she contemplated her daughter's trial, still months away. Another jury on another day in another place would hear much of the same testimony that helped convict Maurice, and the death penalty had remained a possibility for her daughter.

But noting jurors needed only minutes to decide Maurice should not be eligible for capital punishment, Ed Parkinson in early May announced there was no need to subject a second jury to the same emotional toll attached to it. The state would not be seeking the death penalty for Amanda.

Amanda learned of the decision during a visit with her mother and grandmother and felt like celebrating the first good news she had received since her arrest. Relatives of the dead children, however, viewed the coming trial as their chance to lock Amanda in a prison cell and throw away the key, just like her boyfriend.

The state's decision meant Steve Skelton would be back to a solo position as Amanda's defense lawyer. There would be no co-counsel to assist him now that the case carried a life term as its most serious punishment.

Even that would be unfair to her daughter, Ann Danison believed. "She is only guilty of not trying to save the kids herself," she told a reporter. "But she also did the right thing by calling 911."

She firmly believed her daughter and her boyfriend had somehow become ensnared in an accident that took the lives of her three precious grandchildren.

At a court hearing several days later, Judge Peters informed lawyers Amanda's trial would begin Oct. 23, 2006, some six months after Maurice's, in Decatur, the blue-collar factory town a half hour south of Clinton where Amanda had spent time in a psych ward.

At a September pre-trial hearing, Amanda looked noticeably stronger and less anxious. She was ready for her side of the story to be placed in front of a jury. Skelton said he was 99.8 percent sure she would testify and nearly as certain Maurice would be called to the witness stand, too.

On the eve of the trial, Parkinson told reporters the state would strongly oppose any offense less than murder for Amanda in much the same way it had argued in Maurice's case.

"We're going all the way—all or nothing," said the prosecutor.

The Macon County courthouse was much older than its counterpart in Bloomington. Seats were like old-fashioned church pews with seating for about 50 people. Large windows let people keep track of weather conditions as fall gave way to winter. Partisan spectators and witnesses were forced to mingle in a much smaller space or work hard to avoid each other outside the courtroom.

Her hair pulled back in a ponytail and wearing a long black dress and white sweater, Amanda was walked down a short stretch of hallway to the courtroom, giving photographers their first opportunity to capture her image since her arrest. Once seated in the courtroom next to Skelton, Amanda broke into tears. She realized she had arrived at her portal to judgment day.

The first day of the trial was consumed by orientation for about 160 potential jurors, providing them basic information about the trial process. Questions were posed to them the following day, queries and responses not substantially different from what the judge and lawyers had heard in Maurice's trial.

Two mothers of young children volunteered how they would handle a similar drowning situation. "I am a mother. I have two boys," one of them said. "I would drown myself before I would leave my children in a car." She was excused from service.

After eight days of interviewing jury candidates one at a time, five women and seven men were selected. The jury's make-up differed from the group that heard Maurice's case. Where most members of his jury were white collar workers for the same insurance company, the all-white Macon County panel had diverse backgrounds, including a stay-at-home mom, a school secretary and a man on sabbatical from his engineering job.

Looking weary and anxious, Amanda stood along with the lawyers and spectators as the jury entered the room. Opening statements were only moments away. Jurors scanned the space filled with family members, reporters and the curious, some they had seen during their questioning, others they were seeing for the first time. They were beginning to realize service on this high-profile case came with some notoriety.

As he had done in Maurice's trial, Simpson opened with the story from his childhood about breaking a neighbor's window with a baseball. The mental state behind a misjudgment, whether it results in shattered glass or the deaths of three children, is worthy of consideration, he said.

Simpson pointed to his head. "What was going on up here when it happened" would be the issue for the jury, he said.

The prosecutor walked jurors through what he described as undisputed facts of the case. Amanda tapped her knee nervously in between wiping away tears that rolled down her cheeks.

Maurice was portrayed once again as the selfish, unfaithful lover who tormented three children while his girlfriend worked and tolerated his bad behavior because "the sex was real good."

Simpson's view of Amanda was no more sympathetic. Her drive to have a man interfered with her role as a mother—to the point that she went along with his plan to kill her children, he explained.

The varying stories Amanda told police would prove her culpability, Simpson said, and it was in her final police interview, one conducted while she was hospitalized, that Amanda "gave a statement that seemed to be the truth."

Amanda claimed "the original plan was to drive the car straight into the water but the plan was aborted because that other car was there," said Simpson, referring to the second car temporarily parked near the water. It was a critical piece of the police theory about the deaths. As he had done in Maurice's trial, Simpson planted the seed that Amanda may not have even been in the car when it went into the lake. And, just as in the first trial, the state would offer no specific evidence to support that theory.

Simpson reminded jurors the state was not required to provide a motive for the alleged murders. And he asked the panel to consider all aspects of Amanda's behavior the night of the drownings.

"Not only is it the actions of Amanda Hamm but her inaction—her errors of omission—that contributed to the deaths of her children," he said.

Simpson had spoken an hour. Now it was Skelton's turn to step before the jury in Amanda's defense.

These children were loved by their mother during the 4,311 days they spent on this earth, he said.

"She loved them from the day they were born to the day they passed away."

These deaths were not intentional, Skelton said. The evidence would show they were the result of "a horrible, horrible, tragic accident that put them in peril—lethal peril" that their mother was ill-equipped to reverse.

Speaking in a soft voice that never moved above a conversational tone, Skelton asked jurors to remember a presumption of innocence belonged to his client, that the burden to prove charges rested at the state's table.

He said the very manner in which police collected their multiple statements from Amanda was the cornerstone of the defense case.

Those statements were packed with theories, Skelton said, placing a fatherly hand on Amanda's back. "My client was confronted and badgered close to the point of being beaten with these theories."

Skelton argued unfortunate circumstances of Amanda's life would point away from the idea she had something to gain by killing her children. More than half the family's financial resources came from public assistance Amanda received as the single mother of three children, benefits she would lose without them.

The theory that Amanda planned to escape with Maurice to St. Louis without her children also was without merit, Skelton said. The move to Missouri was always premised on five people being part of it.

In an ironic twist related to the St. Louis plan, Skelton disclosed the contents of a letter received the week before the trial by a member of Maurice's family. "The woman sitting here was accepted into the housing program," said Skelton. The plan, he said, was to move to a place with enough bedrooms for her entire family.

Maurice and Amanda both cooperated with police, the defense lawyer said, even after it was clear authorities "had formed an opinion that was carved in stone and was never going to change."

Skelton promised jurors the statement Amanda made to investigators while she was at St. Mary's psychiatric unit would receive a lot of attention during the trial.

"The circumstances surrounding that statement are stark and I suggest they will reach out and grab you by the gut," he said.

Even the date of the crucial interview carried emotional baggage. "The bow on this package? It happened to be Kyleigh's birthday."

And Skelton told jurors police flat-out ignored a mechanical feature of the car that was spelled out in the vehicle's owner's manual.

"If the car is not in 'park' and in gear with the key in the 'on' position, and you open the door, then close it, every one of the locks in that vehicle will lock," said Skelton, implying an immediate rescue may have been more difficult than everyone was assuming.

Closing his hour of remarks, Skelton said "the only reasonable, only true, logical and just verdict in this case will be not guilty."

Amanda welcomed the lunch break as a chance to absorb the avalanche of memories piled up by both lawyers. Alone in her cell, she braced herself for what she anticipated would be nasty and harsh testimony from prosecution witnesses.

Chapter Thirty-four

Little had changed with the state's witness list.

The babysitter, the two women who saw Amanda and Maurice swim in a hotel pool, and the woman who mysteriously saw one child standing in the back seat of the car as it sped to the water's edge all made return visits to the witness stand. Their recollections did not vary from Maurice's trial.

When it came time for jurors to hear the 911 call, the same heavy sadness that had weighed on every person in the Bloomington courtroom engulfed jurors and others in Decatur. Amanda and her mother sobbed as the hysterical plea for help resonated throughout the courtroom. One juror shut her eyes and stiffened, as if she were bracing for a barrage of fear and panic.

If prosecutors believed Amanda's trial would be a repetition of their case against Maurice, the third day of testimony suggested some surprises lie ahead.

Detective Rick Hawn went right to the heart of the state's theory in his responses, saying he paid special attention to the condition of the boat ramp. "I knew it was unlikely for a car to slide," he said.

But it was his reply to a question about Amanda's final words over Christopher's body in the hospital's emergency room that raised Skelton from his chair. In Hawn's opinion, Amanda's good-bye to her son was "fake."

Clearly irritated by the detective's choice of words, Skelton demanded a mistrial and asked that the witness be excused from the courtroom while arguments were heard. The jury also left the courtroom.

The detective had injected his personal opinion into his response, Skelton argued, a "reprehensible and intentional" statement that poisoned the views of all 16 jurors.

"The answer was not what I expected," the chief prosecutor, Simpson, admitted but contended a mistrial was not necessary.

As an experienced police officer, Hawn "darn well knows better than to pull a stunt like that before you or any tribunal," Skelton replied.

Judge Peters declined the mistrial request and told Hawn his answers should not include his personal opinions. The jury was told to disregard Hawn's one-word appraisal of Amanda in the emergency room.

Skelton took a deep breath and began his questioning of Hawn, this time focusing his inquiry on an error in Hawn's testimony at Maurice's trial.

Hawn told Skelton the front passenger's window was open about six inches when the car was removed from the water. Skelton read from a transcript of the previous trial in which Hawn said the window was mostly open.

"I was mistaken, yes sir," Hawn said of his earlier testimony.

The defense also elicited admissions from the detective that he had never before followed a relative into a hospital room as they said their final good-byes. And he conceded he considered Amanda a suspect in a crime before midnight on Sept. 2.

Prosecutors were dealt a second surprise when they called Amanda's friend, Beverly Clymer, to the stand. Far less anxious than she appeared in the first trial, Clymer added a new detail to her previous testimony. She now calmly claimed Amanda had told her about an argument at the lake, a disagreement over Maurice's recurring infidelity.

The story about a quarrel had not appeared in police reports or other sources, Skelton noted.

Prosecutor Parkinson later acknowledged he was hearing Clymer's story for the first time. "But that doesn't mean it isn't true," he said. The people connected with the case were deeply affected by the loss of three children "so what's wrong with their emotions coming through?" Parkinson asked reporters after Clymer's testimony.

The trial took still another unexpected path on the seventh day of testimony when the state agreed to interrupt its case to accommodate the schedules of two defense witnesses, a detour that ultimately proved strategically beneficial for Skelton.

His first defense expert was Dr. Terry Killian, a psychiatrist who had extensively interviewed Amanda and was now testifying just ahead of the state's key witnesses.

Killian educated the jury on the concept of false confessions, how he believed the interview at St. Mary's Hospital was not voluntary on Amanda's part. His psychological tests concluded Amanda was no more likely than most people to lie, but her traumatic past made her susceptible to saying things just to avoid conflict.

Reading from notes on a hospital admission form, Killian quoted Amanda as saying she "just wanted to die, children died Sept. 2 and Sept. 3, boyfriend tried to kill them all and intentionally threw the car in the lake."

Michael Varat, the engineer who helped the defense with automotive tests at a California lake, was the other defense witness to testify during the state's interrupted case. He narrated a video that showed two divers leaving the vehicle as Maurice and Amanda had described, with one exiting through the driver's door and the passenger crawling out the front window. A stuntman's foot got caught as he left the car, a possibility the engineer doubted before it actually occurred during the test.

Varat also explained how the locks operated once the doors were shut and the car was in gear. Varat's technical jargon may have irritated Simpson, but it was not lost on the juror who worked as an engineer. He nodded his head in understanding during Varat's testimony.

In his final question in his cross-examination of Varat, Simpson asked how much his firm had billed taxpayers "for the movie that you made." Varat said the bills would total about $200,000.

As the state resumed its case and the trial moved into a fourth week, the relationship between prosecutors showed signs of strain. Parkinson, who spent much of his professional career handling murder trials, was becoming increasingly frustrated with the long list of additional witnesses Simpson planned to call. "They won't even be able to remember who said what by the end of the trial," Parkinson mumbled as he left court one afternoon.

The effort to keep witnesses lined up in the hallway or on call required coordination that sometimes fell short of the judge's expectation. In his vigilant protection of jurors' time, Judge Peters insisted the trial stay on schedule. Witnesses grumbled when they had to wait. Lawyers moaned when they were unable to produce their next witness.

Sheriff Massey introduced the audio tape of the phone message Amanda left for her family nearly two months after the drownings. Jurors strained to listen as a very distressed woman acknowledged she will never be able to forgive herself for her failures as a mother. The fractured relationship between Amanda and her family also came through for jurors.

A psychiatric social worker shared portions of the notes she took after Amanda came to the Decatur hospital's emergency room as a suicide risk: "I should have left him long ago; attracted to men like this in the past; physically and sexually abusive."

Another chart written by a registered nurse read: "Patient said she thinks she knew her boyfriend wanted to get rid of the kids; patient wants to die; children died Sept. 2.

Patrick Woodcock, a burly male nurse wearing a t-shirt promoting the heavy metal band "Army of Darkness," agreed to read his notes only after assurances from lawyers that he would not be violating patient confidentiality. The patient was depressed and concerned about the interview with the sheriff, said the nurse. Amanda remained on 15-minute suicide watch.

Hospital staffers also checked on Amanda during the breaks in her lengthy meeting with police. "If she wanted to stop the interview, it was done—then and there," the male nurse said. "She was told she didn't have to talk to them."

Dr. Rohidas Patil, the psychiatrist who allowed police to talk to Amanda, told jurors he let Amanda decide if she wanted to speak with the investigators. "I did not feel it was detrimental," the doctor said of his patient's meeting with police.

Paperwork the psychiatrist signed approved "just talking to her, not interrogation," Skelton clarified during his questioning. The defense lawyer went on to ask the psychiatrist whether he would have granted permission if aggressive questioning including the phrase "lying, murderous bitch" were anticipated.

"I wouldn't talk to my patients that way, no matter who it is," Patil replied.

At the end of the day, Skelton offered reporters a prediction of what the prosecution's next witness, state police Master Sergeant Ben Halloran, would reveal to the jury.

Details of more interviews with the defendant, Skelton suggested, and "they will show the revolting manner in which Amanda Hamm was treated."

Chapter Thirty-five

With Dr. Killian's theory about false confessions fresh on jurors' minds, Halloran took the witness chair. It was clear from the state's first question that prosecutors were aware tactics police used to get Amanda's statements could be as significant as what she said.

Halloran testified he knew Amanda was medicated but that she didn't seem impaired during the Sept. 22 interview at St. Mary's Hospital. His report of the meeting was prepared from his written notes that he later shredded, a practice that followed state police policy, he said.

Jurors took their own notes as Halloran laid out the incriminating statements Amanda offered in the interview.

"I knew Maurice was planning an accident, but I didn't know what kind," Halloran quoted Amanda as saying. The state police investigator acknowledged he threatened to end the session when he felt Amanda was not being forthcoming, but he rejected any claim that he called her a cold, murderous bitch during the hospital interview. Asked if he suggested any details Amanda should repeat back to him, Halloran said "not at all."

It was hard not to notice Halloran's imposing stature as he sat at the front of the courtroom. He admitted his tone grew accusatory in exchanges with Amanda. And yes, he acknowledged, she was a suspect at that point.

The lack of an electronic record of what went on behind the closed doors of that small room in St. Mary's psych ward was something Skelton wanted Halloran to explain to the jury.

Was there a reason orders from Simpson to record all interviews were somehow not followed?

"We would listen to the direction of the prosecutor in any case," Halloran responded, but leaving and returning to the sequestered psych ward was a hassle that could delay the interview process. When the topic of getting the recorder from the car came up later, the decision was made to proceed without it, said the witness.

"I made the decision not to record that interview," said Halloran.

Skelton paused, letting the investigator's admission settle across the courtroom. In that silence fell an unspoken suspicion that police preferred not to record Amanda's exact words.

In his questioning of Halloran, Skelton gave jurors a lesson in one of the more controversial methods used by police in interviews with suspects. The "Reid Technique" begins with a cop telling the suspect there's no doubt about his guilt and is provided two explanations for what happened—one more socially acceptable than the other. But in either scenario, the person is admitting guilt.

Jurors saw firsthand how the Reid Technique worked as a 45-minute video of the Sept. 10 interview with Amanda was shown. The accusations leveled by the two female detectives and Halloran's sternly worded warning to Amanda that the world would judge her harshly as a mother resounded through the courtroom.

Halloran testified he had one goal during the multiple interviews. "My goal was the truth. If she was involved, I wanted the details," he said.

Halloran admitted that during their quest for the truth, police had misled Amanda about the evidence authorities had compiled against her. The claim that a security camera was recording everything at the lake Sept. 2 and that blood tests would show how long the children had been in the water were both lies, he confessed to the jury.

The judge allowed Amanda to leave the courtroom when she became visibly upset halfway through the video. Amanda's hysteria and confusion displayed on the tape during the interview was not lost on jurors. They looked tired and emotionally drained as they left the courtroom for the day.

Surrounded by reporters who crowded into the cramped space outside the courtroom for the daily briefing, Skelton promised more evidence of a forced and false confession.

The Sept. 10 interview was disturbing, he said, but the four-hour Sept. 17 video would be even more condemning of police tactics—a real horror show, he said.

"It will be like Bambi meeting Freddy Krueger when you get to the Sept. 17th interview."

When the trial reconvened, Halloran resumed his place in the witness chair for a third and most uncomfortable day of testimony. The detective sat stone-faced as the four-hour audio tape of the Sept. 17 interview was played. His double-proposition question to Amanda near the end of the interview about what should happen to a woman in a bad spot with her boyfriend fit Dr. Killian's tutorial perfectly.

Jurors heard investigators use every tool at their disposal, including the legally acceptable tactic of lying about evidence, to move Amanda from what they perceived to be her denial to admitting she killed her children. It was straight from the Reid Technique playbook.

The undercurrent of discord between members of the prosecution team had swirled with the decision to play the interviews. Parkinson worried their depictions of a shattered mother being brow beaten by detectives would benefit the defense. He also fretted over how the scheduling fluke that put two defense witnesses in the middle of the state's case had probably impugned it.

At that moment, Parkinson would just as well be anywhere but the Macon County courtroom. So, when he was invited by producers of ABC News 20/20 to go to New York for an interview about another case he had handled, he accepted. At her second murder trial in 2006, Julia Rea-Harper had been exonerated of the 1997 murder of her 10-year-old son.

Jurors noticed Parkinson's absence but were unaware the tension churning the prosecution table was also now absent from the courtroom.

Meanwhile, Sheriff Massey was called for a repeat appearance to walk the jury through the automotive tests done by police at the lake.

The malfunction of the car's locking system was recognized on Sept. 6 after Hawn was locked out of the car during the testing at the lake, the sheriff acknowledged to Skelton. Hawn's comment on the video, "We're locked out. What do we do now?" confirmed the door issue, Massey agreed.

Skelton also pressed Massey on Maurice's statement that he could hear the tires spinning. Skelton suggested the state's own video showed that once the car got far enough in the water, while in reverse, the tires would spin.

"You could see some slippage," the sheriff confirmed.

Massey stayed put on the witness stand as another recording, this one of the Sept. 18 questioning at the sheriff's department, was played for jurors. Ann Danison covered her ears during parts of the interview where her daughter described the horrific moments as the car nosedived into the lake.

There also were questions for the sheriff about why a tape recorder never made it into the hospital. The device was left in the trunk to avoid a potential confrontation with hospital staff, he said.

"We weren't very welcome on that floor by medical staff," said Massey.

Once the interview with Amanda got rolling, he said, the decision was made by Halloran and himself to keep things moving. "We don't like to stop and then introduce a recording device," he explained.

The lack of a video or audio record of the seven-hour meeting was regrettable, he conceded. "I wish we had recorded this," he said.

Mark Murphy, the state police polygrapher who accompanied investigators to St. Mary's, was the state's final witness. Unlike his counterparts with the state police, Murphy had retained his notes from the interview and relied on them for his testimony.

In Murphy's version of Amanda's statement, he had her saying that she was "fighting and kicking" as Maurice held her back from the water. Her assertion—an entirely new one from Amanda—that Maurice kept young Austin from opening the car door to escape was personally troubling to Murphy.

"I lost my attention briefly. I thought of my own kids," he said.

More than pleased with Murphy's damning revelation, Simpson scanned the jury box to assess its impact. He hoped for revulsion. Skelton looked unfazed at the defense table as he added Murphy's recollection to the stack of statements police were unable to corroborate with any recording of the interview.

A soft-spoken Notre Dame graduate who had been with the state police for 26 years, Murphy conceded he and Halloran had different personalities that may have surfaced during the interview. "His motor runs a little faster than mine," Murphy said. But he insisted Amanda had been treated respectfully.

After 11 days and 40 witnesses, the state rested its case against Amanda Hamm.

Chapter Thirty-six

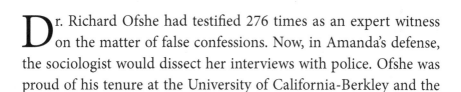

D r. Richard Ofshe had testified 276 times as an expert witness on the matter of false confessions. Now, in Amanda's defense, the sociologist would dissect her interviews with police. Ofshe was proud of his tenure at the University of California-Berkley and the success he had achieved as a nationally recognized expert in his specialized field.

"False confession is a relatively rare phenomena," he said. A self-satisfied demeanor emerged as he used layman's language to explain the concept.

"It's one of the major causes of miscarriages of justice," Ofshe told jurors. "The one and only goal of such an interrogation is to get someone who says, 'I didn't commit the crime' to decide to shift, to move from denial and give it up and give a confession."

Ofshe left the witness stand and stepped to an easel holding illustrations that provided a visual explanation on how a person could be motivated to make a false confession. The confidence of an individual who believes she is innocent of a crime can be shaken, he said, often by interrogators suggesting her situation will improve if she just admits guilt.

"It's not a level playing field. An investigator has all the power."

He said the license police have to lie to suspects also gives authorities an unfair advantage, leading to criminal charges based on false statements. And to offer counseling as an alternative to criminal charges "is more than controversial," Ofshe said. "It's wrong."

A juror who had said during the selection process that he liked to debate nodded in acknowledgement as Ofshe went over the tenets of the Reid Technique of interrogation.

Turning to his review of Amanda's statements, Ofshe noted how recordings of her statements were helpful. A lack of them, he said, put anyone judging the case at a disadvantage.

He said police had used coercive tactics throughout their interaction with Amanda, beginning with threats to send her to prison for a long time if she didn't agree to their version of the incident.

Clearly irritated by the testimony, Simpson asked the judge to strike Ofshe's remarks.

"It's meaningless. He's given us Interrogation 101," Simpson said in an argument that failed to persuade the judge.

Simpson's cross-examination began with an inquiry into the psychologist's lucrative lifestyle. Ofshe listed San Francisco and Paris as places he lived with properties in Arizona, Oregon and the Virgin Islands, too. He was paid $250 an hour for his work on the case, Ofshe said.

Simpson asked the expert if he had read statements provided to police by Amanda's friends and others that differed from what she had told police. Ofshe had not read them. They weren't relevant to what he was hired to do, he said.

Skelton was satisfied that the defense had made headway with Ofshe's testimony on false confessions. The defense lawyer was well aware of the uphill climb facing him with jurors who likely had never thought about the if–why–and–how of deliberately giving a false and incriminating statement to police. But he believed his expert had bridged the knowledge gap.

Psychologist Dr. Mark Cunningham was called to share an assessment of Amanda similar to what he had offered at Maurice's trial. He found Amanda no more qualified than her boyfriend to react to the crisis at the lake.

Amanda wiped away tears as Cunningham shared the traumas of her childhood and intellectual limitations that had left her especially vulnerable. When the psychologist disclosed her IQ as a low average of 82, Amanda turned to Skelton and asked, "Does that mean I'm retarded?" No, her lawyer assured her, it did not.

Cunningham had learned a great deal about Amanda in three interviews he conducted with her at the jail late in 2005 and early in 2006. Rejected by her peers and sexually abused by several men, Amanda sought and found one source for love, Cunningham testified. "Motherhood was her only source of positive identity and security."

In his assessment of Maurice, Cunningham agreed with others' conclusions that Maurice was unfaithful to his partners and left them when he became bored. When it came to Amanda's children, Maurice "teased way too hard"—a practice that didn't seem to frighten them, Cunningham offered.

In the months since Maurice's trial, Simpson had not warmed to Cunningham's conclusions. But Parkinson, back in the courtroom now, was concerned an aggressive cross examination of the openly friendly witness would be counter-productive.

As he had done with Ofshe, Simpson asked Cunningham about his fees, hoping jurors would question the credibility of what they were hearing. The cases had been worth about $80,000 for his 300 hours of work, Cunningham said.

Understanding how distance can be difficult for some people to visualize, Simpson stood along a wall of the courtroom to show jurors what 26.5 feet—the distance between the car's rear bumper and the water's edge—looked like. He went on to ask the psychologist to explain what the prosecutor considered Amanda's lack of maternal instincts to save her children.

"What she did with her maternal feelings was run to the phone," Cunningham responded.

After a long day of testimony focusing on psychological elements of the case, Skelton told reporters his goal was to give jurors an unembroidered view of Amanda and Maurice and the baggage they had carried since childhood, leaving them limited abilities to manage day-to-day responsibilities, let alone a life-or-death crisis. Just because the couple would never be compared to the long-ago TV couple Ozzie and Harriett did not make them murderers, he said.

The next day, Maurice's half-sister Shamika Jefferson recounted Maurice's phone call to her about the drownings.

"You could barely make out what he was saying," she said. "He was so distraught and crying uncontrollably. I have not seen him that distraught since our mother passed."

She recounted how the LaGrone family drove to Clinton to deliver sympathy cards and money collected for Amanda and her family. "My heart went out to Amanda. I could see her pain. She was weak with grief," said Jefferson.

She testified how high tension expressed through racial remarks in the community helped convince Maurice's relatives to return to St. Louis ahead of the funeral.

"Because of everything that was in the air, we made a conscious decision not to attend," she said. She said comments overheard by family members were both offensive and hurtful to Maurice's family.

Maurice was a big, shy kid who liked to play jokes on his cousins, his half-sister said. His childhood nickname of "Boo," an epithet prosecutors had linked to his misguided pranks, was given him by his father who considered "Baby Boo" to be beautiful, she explained.

Maurice's stepmother, Betty March, told jurors how she worried about the cavernous depression that swallowed Maurice and Amanda after the drownings. After they came to stay with her and Maurice's father, she asked them to accompany her to her cleaning jobs, just to get them out of the house. Amanda rarely ate and paced the floor during the two weeks she was with the family.

"She said she panicked and it was an accident. Then she left us and that was it," said March.

Amanda's stepfather Mark Walston told jurors the possibility that interviews with police could lead to the devastating legal consequences that eventually hit his adopted daughter was always in the back of his mind.

In the weeks after his grandchildren drowned, Walston contacted three lawyers about her situation. "It wasn't my decision to make. I suggested she should have an attorney, but I left it up to her," Walston said.

When he became aware police were going to speak with Amanda at St. Mary's, Walston called an attorney who advised him that "she would look guilty if she had an attorney." Still, his gut instinct told him the meeting could have negative consequences for his daughter.

Ann Danison's anxiety shadowed her to the witness stand. She drew a deep breath and let it go before summoning the strength to once again share details of the last time she saw her grandchildren. Several jurors wept as she forced each sentence from somewhere deep inside her, from a place where precious memories were still competing with sharp-edged grief. Emotions ran just as high as the first time she answered similar questions at Maurice's trial.

The loss of the three children had left a gaping hole in everyone's life. "They were her life. They were my life," Danison said in response to inquiries about Amanda's dedication as a mother.

She admitted the failure of Amanda and Maurice to save her grandchildren had angered her. The end result of that failure and the convincing opinions of police that Amanda and Maurice were guilty initially made it possible for her to condemn the pair.

At the end of her cross examination by Simpson, Danison acknowledged there appeared to be negative things going on in

Amanda's life with Maurice that she didn't know about. "She didn't confide in me," Amanda's mother said.

The male nurse assigned to look after Amanda during breaks in her long hospital interview was asked about a tape recorder he recalled seeing in Halloran's hands. Patrick Woodcock's memory seemed to dim in the year since his defense deposition when he recalled seeing the device.

"At this point, I don't know who had what," said Woodcock in his reply to Skelton's question aimed at raising doubt about a critical element of the police interview.

To fortify the jury's impression of the nurse's weakened memory, Skelton called Kendra Moses, a social worker with the Illinois Public Defender's Office, to talk about her interview with Woodcock. They, too, had talked about audio and video equipment, she said.

The nurse had told Moses that when Murphy came to the hospital, he "had his polygraph equipment." That statement caused Simpson to cough loudly in a deliberate attempt to muffle the reference to a polygraph. The results of so-called lie detector tests are barred as evidence, making any discussion of them prohibited by witnesses.

"Sorry," said Moses, before she went on to confirm her recollection that Woodcock stated he had seen a small tape recorder in the hands of a detective who came to interview Amanda.

Skelton was satisfied with the information he had laid in jurors' laps, information consistent with Amanda's recollection that a tape recorder had indeed been brought into the room, prompting a question of whether one had been turned on.

The question as to whether Amanda would testify was resolved with Skelton's disclosure to the judge that she would not be taking the witness stand. After many sleepless nights mulling the possible benefits and downfalls, Skelton opted to keep her in her chair next to him and out of the state's clutches.

So after more than five weeks of testimony, the defense was ready to close its case with a 30th witness. Kathy Madix was Christopher's kindergarten teacher.

The 6-year-old boy was a gentle, caring kid with "a smile that made you want to smile back," she said. Madix noticed no changes in Christopher after Maurice moved into the household. Nor did she recall ever seeing Maurice at the school.

To those in the courtroom who loved the little boy, Madix's testimony was another raw reminder of the sweet and loving nature of the child they had lost. For the defense, the teacher's recollection offered useful rebuttal to accusations that Maurice had a negative impact on Amanda's children.

Prosecutors then asked to be allowed to present rebuttal evidence to Michael Varat's automotive testimony by sharing portions of a television interview Maurice gave to a local station three months earlier. Maurice's statements about how the accident happened were based on a theory crafted with the help of his lawyers, argued Simpson.

"It's impeachment. He's saying 'I don't know what happened and we kind of made it up,'" he said.

Judge Peters denied Simpson's request and agreed with Skelton's objection that the interview had been edited. And since Maurice wouldn't be testifying, he couldn't be asked about it. The series of stinging reactions Maurice had lobbed at Simpson during his testimony at his own trial was a mistake Skelton was unwilling to let Maurice repeat at Amanda's. The defense lawyer had a good feeling about how things were going and saw no reason to take unnecessary risks.

The move to keep both defendants from testifying did not surprise Parkinson. Besides, he believed jurors heard Amanda's side of the story through the testimony of multiple police officers. "Her word did get out, as far as what happened," Parkinson told reporters.

Skelton agreed. But in his view, Amanda's story was based on a different premise: "Her position is 'I would not do anything to hurt my kids. I did not do anything to hurt my kids.'"

For the state and prosecution, the next hurdle would come with instructions jurors would receive for their deliberations. Once again, the state viewed the case as an all-or-nothing proposition with no room for a verdict on a lesser offense.

Skelton had a decision to make. Should he bet on an acquittal on murder charges or ask for a less serious alternative?

Maurice's jury had offered a lesson on the value of options.

Chapter Thirty-seven

Under myriad provisions of the law, a person can be convicted of a crime other than the one he or she was accused of. If things have gone well for the defense, the conviction can be for a less serious crime, one the judge believes may have been an element of the more dire accusation. Jurors weren't present when lawyers in Amanda's case gathered in the courtroom to hash out instructions the judge would give the panel. Each side had curve balls ready to pitch.

Parkinson wanted jurors to assume a mother was legally responsible for protecting her children from harm, an argument Skelton had never heard before.

"A parent may not sit idly by and do nothing," claimed Parkinson.

The prosecutor cited several witness statements and the quote police attributed to Amanda in which she told Maurice she "wanted to play with her kids first."

"Before what? How about murder?" Parkinson scoffed. "We're claiming she wasn't even in the car. She failed to protect her kids, and we feel the evidence will support that she knew what was going to happen when they went to the lake."

Judge Peters allowed the simply-worded phrase "a parent has a duty to protect her child" to be part of the jury instructions.

The defense had a surprise of its own. Skelton asked that child endangerment, a lesser offense than murder, be an option the jury could consider.

The judge explained to Amanda that she didn't have to go along with Skelton's request for the added option, a charge that could result in a sentence ranging from probation to 20 years in prison. When directly asked about the child endangerment option, Amanda told the judge, "Go with that one."

Prosecutor Simpson couldn't fathom how a reasonable juror could settle on a child endangerment conviction in place of murder charges. That, he said, would require jurors to view Amanda's conduct as simply a matter of parental negligence.

After hearing all the evidence in the case, it was possible jurors could conclude the children's deaths were, in fact, an accident, Skelton's seven-page memorandum in support of the jury option read. And even if they believed Maurice was guilty of murder, they could still find Amanda wasn't accountable for his actions, Skelton argued.

Prosecutors seemed caught off-guard by Skelton's request and supporting memorandum. Their arguments against the less-than-murder charge were relatively brief. Judge Peters seemed easily persuaded by Skelton's pleading. The jury would have that option.

With the hearing over, Parkinson vented his displeasure to reporters.

"Not to be lost in this trial are the three little kids who should be celebrating Christmas," he said. Yes, he admitted, the child endangerment request was a surprise.

Skelton told reporters he was ready to seek an involuntary manslaughter option if Peters had turned down child endangerment.

He also previewed his closing argument.

"I will argue that Christopher, Austin and Kyleigh were loved every day of their lives and were not the object of any conceived or perceived ill will from Amanda. This was a tragic, tragic accident."

There were predictable reactions from two of the children's grandmothers to the judge's decision that jurors could weigh child endangerment as a possible verdict.

"I don't understand why he'd rule for that option," said Reta Hamm, disappointed Amanda now could be found guilty of something less than murder in the death of her grandson, Christopher.

A late afternoon phone call from Amanda to another grandmother—her mother—was met with optimism.

"Amanda was excited and I'm thrilled," Ann Danison said. "I can live with child endangerment because she didn't save the children."

The courtroom was crowded for closing arguments. State police officers who had worked the cases took positions in the back row. Sheriff Massey sat next to Simpson in the seat normally taken by Ed Parkinson, his absence for the final phase of the trial interpreted by trial watchers as another indication of discord between the prosecutors.

When Simpson stepped in front of the jury for his hour-long argument, he was ready to conclude an assignment involving two murder cases that had lasted more than three years. His opinion of the defendants had not changed.

"If they had an Olympic event for laziness, he'd have the gold medal wrapped around his neck," Simpson said of Maurice, a man he considered "the most self-indulgent person imaginable."

Even Amanda's name could be construed as a symbol of her priorities, said Simpson.

"A man duh," he intoned. "The first four letters of her name are A Man."

Holding up a large photo of the children for all the jurors to see, Simpson walked them through the everyday routine of Amanda's household on Sept. 2, 2003.

"She's creating the illusion she's just out there doing her daily chores," when in fact her actions showed "the creation of a quasi-alibi," said Simpson, his voice dripping with disdain.

Simpson paced nine broad steps across the courtroom to illustrate the distance from the submerged car to the shore.

"There's life inside that vehicle," he said. "The defendant and her addiction are up at the phone making a meaningless and useless 911 call."

As Amanda watched, Simpson said her failure to stay or go back into the water to save her children put her in a unique category as a mother. What sort of mother would fail so badly in the duty to protect her children?

He pointed to Amanda. "That one!"

Skelton placed a supportive hand on Amanda's shoulder, then stood for his closing statement.

In their scrutiny of the evidence and testimony, Skelton asked jurors to consider five witnesses who, he said, all brought personal agendas to the courtroom.

The babysitter Susan Swearingen, so-called best friend Beverly Clymer, and medical workers Linda Stickney, Sondra Moore and Cassandra McFall "shared their attitudes and warped perceptions that were patently false," said Skelton.

The defense lawyer questioned why those who criticized Amanda's parenting skills after the tragedy ⊠ in particular the children's fathers — hadn't intervened beforehand to somehow protect the children if they were at risk.

Because there was a logical explanation for how the car went into the water, the state was short of what it needed to prove murder beyond a reasonable doubt, Skelton argued.

"This case involved tunnel vision and a rush to judgment that didn't take very God darned long," said Skelton, moving on to what he considered the more egregious tactics used by police to make their case.

The issue of whether there was a recording of the police interrogation of Amanda in the psych ward raised doubts about the very veracity of the incriminating statements attributed to her, Skelton argued. A nurse's belief that a recorder made it into the hospital should be considered, he said.

"Maybe the tape wasn't what they wanted to hear."

The closely-analyzed questioning by Sergeant Ben Halloran fit the concepts of a false confession, said Skelton, reading from a portion of the Sept. 17 interview where the suspect was offered a "second chance" by the detective.

"If you can't trust the messenger, you can't trust with certainty the message that's brought into this courtroom," said Skelton.

In his rebuttal, Simpson asked jurors to stay focused on the most serious allegations of the state's case.

Simpson suggested the child endangerment option was born out of a defense hope for something other than a murder conviction. That brought Skelton out of his seat in protest. The judge sustained the objection without explaining why Simpson's remark was inappropriate.

"Don't cheapen this case," Simpson continued, referring to the lesser offense. "Don't compromise the evidence in this case by returning that verdict alone." He was referring to the lesser offense.

Judge Peters sent the jury from the courtroom to begin deliberations. There would be a long vigil for a verdict.

Chapter Thirty-eight

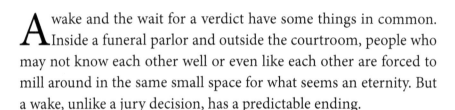

A wake and the wait for a verdict have some things in common. Inside a funeral parlor and outside the courtroom, people who may not know each other well or even like each other are forced to mill around in the same small space for what seems an eternity. But a wake, unlike a jury decision, has a predictable ending.

The children's relatives, still divided by their opinions of the case, stayed apart in separate camps outside the courtroom. A room at the end of the hallway served as a gathering spot for one large group of family members who left their posts only for cigarette and lunch breaks. Even then, they stayed connected through cell phones.

Any forecasts that there would be a quick verdict evaporated as jurors were sent home after a little more than two hours of deliberation.

When they resumed the next morning, they submitted the first of several questions to the judge. Jurors wanted to know if any life insurance policies had been taken out on the children—a query the judge would not answer—and they requested the 911 tape and a transcript of the September 17 interview. Both items were given to them for review.

Lawyers were back in the courtroom on the second day. Skelton was seeking a mistrial. After mulling over Simpson's closing arguments, Skelton decided to make an issue of the prosecutor's comment about the child endangerment option.

"The jury was left with the impression that I was asking or begging for a compromise in this case, and that couldn't be farther from the truth," said Skelton.

Simpson viewed the issue as already resolved. "Whatever error occurred was absolutely nipped in the bud by the objection," said the prosecutor.

Judge Peters declined to declare a mistrial.

Inside the cramped quarters of the jury room, the panel began its work with each juror saying where he or she stood on the issue of guilt or innocence. The group was about evenly split. And so it was decided that the best way to build a consensus was to review discrepancies in witness statements, an exercise that led to extensive discussion of what may have been behind Amanda's failure to save her children. The longest debate churned over whether Amanda's clothing was wet or dry when first responders arrived. Jurors agreed to disagree on the point.

The contradictions of Amanda's personality and her reaction to trauma continued to swirl. Was she a good person who chose the wrong men? Was she a good mother who clung too tightly to the dream of a stable family? Did she allow a boyfriend to talk her into a fatal mistake? Or did she panic and run in an emergency? Those were questions jurors tried to answer to complete their picture of Amanda.

The manner in which police conducted their investigation was more of an issue for some jurors than others, but the refusal by police to videotape Amanda's hospital interview and Detective Halloran's demeanor on the witness stand left doubts in several jurors' minds about the overall inquiry.

The hours dragged on in the dimly lit room. Jurors took few breaks for doughnuts and a trip to the tiny restroom located at one end of the jury quarters. An officer posted outside the door kept watch that no information leaked in or out until a decision was made. Only then would jurors be released.

With little else to do as deliberations continued, waiting people ramped up their speculation on which direction the jury was headed. Reporters joined in the time filler, trying to chat up the lawyers. With the evidentiary part of the trial over, Simpson felt comfortable talking briefly with reporters as he passed them on his walk to a room where he and others connected to the state's case waited.

Growing concerned over the length of the deliberations, his fellow prosecutor, Parkinson, floated a possible settlement past Skelton. Amanda could end the uncertainty by pleading guilty to one count of murder in exchange for a sentence of 20 years, the minimum term for murder in Illinois.

Skelton had no intention of giving the state a guilty plea, an opinion Amanda confirmed after the two conferred about the offer.

The verdict watch began to take on a more casual atmosphere—something that also occurs at wakes when people shift away from the solemn matter that brought them together. Several reporters had brought home-baked cookies to share with anyone who wanted one. Judge Peters sampled some when he stopped to chat on his way to his chambers.

Craig Brown brought his five children to the courthouse, along with a selection of books and puzzles to keep them busy. One of his younger sons passed the time by collecting autographs from anyone who seemed important—including the judge, the sheriff and employees of the circuit clerk's office.

Bored reporters broke out a deck of cards.

Thursday, the third day of deliberations, opened with word from the court administrator that the jurors wanted a lunch option besides the chicken and fries from Wing Zone where they had been taken the past two days. Pizza would be the new option. A reference by jurors to "next week" in their memo about food fueled speculation things would not be settled by the weekend.

On Friday afternoon, another note arrived from the jury: Could Amanda Hamm be guilty of first-degree murder if she knew Maurice LaGrone planned to kill the children but was unaware of specifics of that plan, including knowing the car was going into the water?

The judge would not allow a response to the inquiry, instead directing jurors to rely on his instructions. Later the same day, the jury asked to see Dr. Ofshe's diagram on false confessions.

If the defense and state were able to draw any inference from the jury request, they didn't share them. But it seemed clear at least some jurors had doubts about Amanda's role in the deaths. Indeed, the number of jurors unconvinced of Amanda's guilt was growing.

After another full day of talks Monday, Dec. 11, the jury went home without having posed any new questions or requests to the court. Ann Danison said she tried to keep her mind off the deliberations by cleaning house. She had brought Amanda's winter coat to protect her from the 45-degree temperature should the verdict go her way. Danison also carried two pieces of paper. They contained media statements prepared for the potential verdicts.

"This is a happy day for our family after more than three years of overwhelming sorrow," said the statement prepared for an acquittal on murder charges. Accompanying a guilty verdict would be a family statement that "the loss of our grandchildren continues to be compounded by the bias and prejudice of those who are interested in their personal agendas."

The bars on the windows of the jury room became emblematic of the growing despair and weariness of the 12 people charged with deciding Amanda's fate. Five days of talks had produced no unanimous decision on the murder charge. Jurors who favored a guilty of murder verdict sensed no hope that more discussion would bring the three jurors who supported a not guilty verdict to their side. Finally, those convinced of Amanda's guilt agreed to accept a guilty verdict on the child endangerment charge if it would break the gridlock.

The verdict was accepted with little discussion.

On mid-Tuesday afternoon, the jury signaled it was ready with a verdict.

Police officers, including state police investigators Ben Halloran and Val Panizo, packed the back row on the defense side of the courtroom. The three alternate jurors, dismissed at the start of deliberations when their service was no longer needed, came back for the final outcome and also found seats in the crowded courtroom.

As jurors filed into the courtroom, Amanda looked straight ahead, her arms folded across her chest as if she were binding her nerves, hopes and prayers tightly together. She began to cry as the judge cautioned spectators that outbursts would not be tolerated.

Jury foreman Paul Taussig handed the envelope containing verdict forms to the clerk. She passed it to the judge. Peters looked through the paperwork and read aloud the one piece that mattered:

"We the jury find Amanda Hamm guilty of endangering the life and health of Christopher Hamm, Austin Brown, and Kyleigh Hamm."

Amanda turned to Skelton. "What do we do now?" she asked, struggling to process the reality that she had been acquitted of murdering her children.

Cradling her face in his hands, Skelton said, "We'll get through this. Be strong."

The strict rules for courtroom demeanor kept reactions to the verdict heavily restrained until the proceedings were adjourned. But smiles from Amanda's family members and tight grimaces from police offices and relatives of the children left no doubt about how people viewed the verdict.

With the acquittal on murder charges, Skelton saw no reason bond should remain at the $5 million set three years earlier. A bond of $15,000 that would require Amanda to post $1,500 should be sufficient, he argued.

The judge agreed to reduce the bond to $100,000—or $10,000 for the purposes of posting the cash needed for her release. Fully aware that every day Amanda had already been incarcerated would count towards her ultimate sentence, the family opted not to stretch their resources to raise the money. Amanda would remain in jail for the 51 days before her Feb. 1 sentencing in which she could receive anything from probation to 20 years in prison.

Standing before a crowd that included prosecutors, lawyers and police officers, four jurors agreed to return to the courtroom after the verdicts to talk to reporters.

Juror Diane Bowers read a statement that the verdict "was based upon the evidence presented to us and very, very careful deliberations."

Beads of perspiration glistened on Simpson's forehead.

"I accept the verdict, but I'm not satisfied with it. Despite the state's disappointment, the system worked," he said. In his view, the option to vote for something other than murder gave the jury a path to compromise.

Police who investigated the case were shocked by the verdict and left the courtroom with long faces. It was only partial justice for the children, Sheriff Massey said, adding "we know a lot about the case the jury didn't get to hear."

In a brief conversation with her mother, Amanda tried to reassure family members, saying she was optimistic about her life for the first time in more than three years.

"Mom, it's okay," she said. "I still have my life ahead of me. It's not murder."

Maurice, meanwhile, was still in the Macon County jail, waiting for the testimony he was never called to give. When word got to him that Amanda had been acquitted of the murder charges, he was pleased. In a phone call to his stepmother, he said he hoped for the best for his former girlfriend.

Fathers and other relatives of the children felt the lack of a murder conviction betrayed three young lives. They were angry.

Standing in a parking lot outside the courthouse, Greg Hamm displayed his rage. As Ann Danison and others passed by, he held up a photo of his son, Christopher.

"He's what she murdered," he said.

Chapter Thirty-nine

In fact, Amanda's verdict was not well received by many people — most especially by those in Clinton who had convinced themselves long ago that what was good for Maurice was equally good for Amanda.

The word "nigger" was not quoted in their stories, but reporters who visited bars and coffee shops searching for reaction frequently heard the racial slur when people talked about Amanda's relationship with Maurice.

An appeal of the child endangerment conviction was on Steve Skelton's agenda. But first he had to prepare for Amanda's sentencing hearing just six weeks away.

The more than a thousand days she had already served would be fair punishment for Amanda's mistake, he planned to tell Judge Peters. Meanwhile an online campaign seeking support for the maximum sentence of 20 years was organized by the dead children's relatives. Their petition was forwarded to the judge along with several victim impact statements.

The DeWitt County courtroom where the Hamm-LaGrone cases had begun three years earlier was packed with an audience awaiting the final step in the quest for justice they had been following since the children died.

Predictably, the state asked for the full 20 years.

Ann Danison was called by Roger Simpson and asked her opinion as to what justice her grandchildren deserved. It was an impossible question, she felt, one that demanded she separate her love for Christopher, Austin and Kyleigh from that of her daughter, something she couldn't do.

But she did share the change she had witnessed in Amanda.

"She's paid the ultimate price by losing her three kids because of abuse, and she's finally come to accept how she needs to change her life," Amanda's mother testified.

In his final statement, Simpson disagreed with that observation.

"Amanda Hamm has not paid the ultimate price. Her children paid the ultimate price."

When it came time to offer her statement, Amanda read from two pages she had prepared. She began with her regrets.

"I regret that I formed a relationship with Maurice LaGrone, not because he was an evil person, but because he was immature, selfish and unwilling to be a responsible partner. He contributed little to our little 'family' financially and was more concerned about his wants and needs than those of others," she read. Her words were soft-spoken and deliberate as she focused on each word in front of her as if her life depended upon it.

She had held out hope that her boyfriend would grow up; it never happened. She pledged to avoid similar mistakes in future relationships.

Amanda found tragic irony in that she could try to rebuild her life after her release from prison. Her children "no longer have similar horizons to look forward to," she acknowledged.

The judge reviewed several scenarios he had heard during the two trials where Maurice physically and emotionally abused the children. "These were three children who had no means of defending themselves," he said.

A shock wave rippled through the courtroom when the judge announced his decision: 10 years in prison, with credit for the slightly more than three years already served in jail. With customary and expected day-for-day credit for good behavior, Amanda could be free in three or four years.

Disbelief gave way to anger in the courthouse lobby. Several relatives quickly left before their emotions boiled over in front of television cameras. Austin's father stayed and fumed about Amanda's decision to break her silence in the courtroom.

"She came in here to try to get the very least amount of sentence possible. Then she speaks up," said Craig Brown.

Prosecutor Parkinson let his opinions roll as well.

"This case is about three dead children," he said. "It's not about all that scientific crap we've heard the last three years. I'm disappointed in the verdict and the sentence."

The lingering disgust many local residents had carried since Amanda's conviction on the lesser charge erupted with the sentence. Their comments to reporters and to one another as they mulled the judge's decision over beers at Clinton's watering holes reflected strong opinions that Amanda's punishment was far too lenient. Jury and judge, be damned, they said.

Meanwhile the LaGrone defense team was shifting its hopes to the possibility that the appellate court would order a new trial for Maurice.

Stuart Shiffman, a lawyer with the State Appellate Defender's office, would oversee the appeal with its claim that Judge Peters erred when he refused to give the jury the second verdict option he had allowed in Amanda's case.

In January 2008, the appellate court upheld Maurice's conviction, saying the trial judge was correct when he rejected involuntary manslaughter as a possible verdict: No evidence had been offered to support a theory that attempting to back up the ramp was a reckless act.

Amanda by then had settled into the routine at the Dwight Correctional Center, less than an hour from the prison where Maurice would likely spend the rest of his life. She decided against an appeal.

Writing on her behalf in August of that year, her lawyer said that "because this was a lengthy, complex case that generated strong opinions in the community, I do not want to subject myself, or the State, to another trial in this matter and thus do not want to pursue any trial issues in my case no matter how viable."

A month later, in September of 2008, Amanda left prison, having served about 19 months at Dwight. Her family picked her up in front of a handful of reporters who traveled to the prison 90 miles northeast of Clinton to see her set free after almost five years behind bars. Her next step was a halfway house. While there, she sent photos of herself to Maurice in prison.

DeWitt County Public Defender Richard Goff—the same lawyer who was asked to give Amanda advice in the early stages of the police investigation—helped Maurice prepare another motion for a new trial in early 2009.

The paperwork included an admission from one of Maurice's attorneys, Jeff Justice, that he made a mistake when he didn't pursue child endangerment as a possible verdict. He had wrongly believed the lesser charge couldn't apply because Maurice wasn't a parent or legal guardian.

Ed Parkinson bristled at the notion of Maurice getting a second trial. "He was convicted for murder, and that's what we tried him on, and that's what the jury found," he said.

The request for a new trial was rejected by Judge Garry Bryan, appointed to the bench after Judge Peters' retirement. He found no other Illinois cases where a judge had allowed child endangerment as a lesser option for jurors to consider while murder remained a possible verdict. Judge Bryan ruled it was proper to deny jurors the option of finding the defendant guilty of the less serious charge because child endangerment was not viewed as a factor or element of the more serious charge, a ruling later affirmed by the Fourth District Appellate Court.

When the Illinois Supreme Court refused to hear Maurice's case in July 2010, it appeared every avenue of legal review that could change his fate had been explored and—with no new evidence or compelling legal argument coming from a seasoned lawyer—sealed.

Chapter Forty

One of the first trips Amanda made after her release from prison was to Clinton's cemetery to visit the graves of her children. Seeing their names etched on the grey stone grave markers drew her to her knees. There was a rush of renewed grief and a need to be close to them once more.

Amanda's time in her hometown was brief and guarded.

When she went shopping with her mother, she stayed in the car, afraid of the stares and snarls she would surely encounter if she were recognized. She knew her safety and chances to rebuild her life were far better in Chicago, 170 miles away, where she could be anonymous in a city of almost three million.

Life in the halfway house for women was not ideal but it came with freedom, something Amanda had been denied for five years. She looked forward to the paychecks and tips she earned as a waitress at a restaurant that helped ex-offenders.

Another gap in Amanda's life was filled when she met Leo Ware, a man 11 years her senior. He, too, was starting over. He had a record of drug convictions. Her relationship with a black man was nothing extraordinary in the big city, another reason Chicago was the place to begin this new chapter of Amanda's life.

Leo knew Amanda's three children had died, but some of the details were buried so deeply inside her and caused her such trauma when she relived them that he did not press her for more information. He believed her when she said it was an accident.

To build a future together, Amanda and Leo decided to look forward and let the past remain in the rearview mirror.

She became pregnant about a year after her release while still on parole. The thought of having more children excited her. Her parole agent was aware of the upcoming birth and visited Amanda and her baby girl after she was born in June 2010. A month later, Amanda and Leo were married.

In November 2011, the couple had their second child, another girl.

The start of a new family didn't erase the memory of Amanda's first three children. Photos of Kyleigh, Austin and Christopher were displayed in the Ware home alongside photos of their two daughters.

Amanda kept her job at the restaurant. Leo worked construction when jobs were available. The girls attended a pre-school near their home on Chicago's north side. Finally, life was stable and good. It would prove, however, to be the calm before another storm in Amanda's life.

Pregnant again in February 2014, Amanda was admitted to the same hospital where her two daughters had been born—this time with blood pressure issues just days before her due date.

Amanda's doctor, assigned to her case the previous month, came to her room Feb. 28 with the hospital administrator. Somehow the doctor—whether from a memory of the intense publicity of the drowning case or the marginally true material still available about it on the internet — had recognized Amanda as the mother convicted of playing a part in the deaths of her three children.

"We want to know if you're Amanda Hamm," said the administrator, suggesting that some information already confirmed the hunch.

Amanda acknowledged her identity, stunned it could suddenly be an issue.

The doctor told Amanda she was required to report the impending birth to the Illinois Department of Children and Family Services based on Amanda's criminal record involving the deaths of three children. In an instant, any stability her family knew had vanished. Her new life was about to be darkened by old circumstances.

The next morning, Amanda delivered a healthy baby boy on a day filled with both joy and devastation. When state welfare workers came to the hospital with an investigator, Amanda learned for the first time that her name was on a list of child abusers in the State Central Register. It had been there eight years and was to remain there another 42 years, among those of 23,000 other adults where allegations of child abuse or neglect had been deemed credible by DCFS investigators. That year more than 1,500 children were taken into protective custody in Chicago. Depending on the accusation, people were placed on the list for either five, 20 or 50 years.

The list was not public but was available to law enforcement, doctors, school officials and others who hired people to work with children and with adults with mental disabilities.

What were the consequences of being on such a list? Amanda wondered. Maybe DCFS would monitor her family, she speculated. Not a pleasant thought, but something she could handle for the sake of her children.

The doctor's call to the DCFS hotline jolted the agency. Top-level officials scrambled for a plan that would allow DCFS to avoid the public reprisals that would surely come when people learned that the mother who had been so vilified when her children died in a lake was able to give birth to three more children, all outside the ever-watchful eye of the state's child protection agency.

DCFS was still reeling from the harsh media criticism that occurred after an eight-year-old girl, Gizzelle Ford, had been found beaten and strangled after its investigator failed to spot signs of trouble at the filthy Chicago apartment where Gizzelle lived with her father and grandmother. The father died in jail before he could be tried for the torture death of his daughter. The grandmother, Helen Ford, was convicted of murder and is serving a life term. A jury had awarded $48 million to the girl's family.

Turmoil inside the child welfare agency meant it had seven directors and acting directors in three years' time. Now Amanda Ware represented a potential political and public relations predicament DCFS did not need.

Amanda underwent a basic psychological evaluation in her hospital room. Questions were asked about the drownings.

A social worker was dispatched to the Wares' apartment near Wrigley Field to check on the children and condition of their home. Amanda called Leo to warn him of the unexpected visit. Their two daughters were on an outing with Amanda's mother, visiting from Clinton.

The DCFS worker asked Leo if he knew about his wife's past and the deaths of her children.

"That's between her, her boyfriend, her kids and God," Leo told the worker. "I know the hurt and pain she feels. I see it and live with it every day."

Everything seemed satisfactory to the worker. She called a supervisor to report her findings.

"Take the kids," the supervisor directed over the phone. The social worker was surprised. The order to remove the children was at odds with what workers experienced in other cases where the home and family showed no signs of problems.

Another DCFS worker arrived. They awaited the children's return.

Then it was like a scene from the worst custody battle. Ann Danison tried desperately to calm and comfort her grandchildren, now kicking, screaming and crying as the state workers placed them in a van with nothing more than the clothes they were wearing. Their father stood helpless, attempting to make sense of what seemed to be an impulsive and cruel decision, knowing this was a moment his wailing daughters would likely never forget.

In their Chicago apartment, Amanda and Leo Ware talked about the loss of their three children in September, 2014, seven months after State of Illinois child welfare workers removed the children from their custody. (*The Pantagraph*/David Proeber)

Maurice LaGrone Jr. talked to reporters in a November 2017 visit at the Western Illinois Correctional Center. (Photo by Edith Brady-Lunny)

Greg Hamm, Craig Brown and Shane Senters stood at their children's graves following a memorial service in September, 2018 to mark 15 years since the children drowned in their mother's car. (Photo by Edith Brady-Lunny)

The welfare workers struggled for answers when the grandmother demanded to know why the girls were being taken from their father.

A first step in the DCFS plan was being accomplished by taking custody of the children.

After more horrific moments, the girls were driven away to several hours of exams and tests for signs of abuse. Then they were taken to the home of Leo's sister in Englewood, a south side neighborhood with one of Chicago's highest murder rates.

Two days later Amanda was released from the hospital. It would be three more days before she was allowed to see her newborn son, also now in custody of the state.

The sudden loss of her three children to child welfare workers was psychologically close to her 2003 nightmare. This time, however, she knew her children were alive. She prayed for their safety. She also prayed that the legal system she felt had betrayed her a decade earlier would return her children if she could satisfy its demands.

Meanwhile her husband struggled to understand why the state needed to take his children from him, as well as from their mother. Was it guilt by association, he wondered. Were his children at risk with him because he married a woman with a tragic past, one he felt he fully understood when he vowed to stand by her through the best and worst of times?

A week after the children were taken into DCFS custody, a court hearing determined the next step. Associate Judge Demetrios Kottaras of Cook County's juvenile court told lawyers gathered around two tables with Leo and Amanda that he wanted the parents to visit the children as often as possible.

With scant information about the 2003 case, the judge complimented the couple on their ability to overcome strong adversities—even calling them a success story. The problem, the judge told Amanda, was that he wanted to make sure she was over the trauma of burying three children.

The state's demands started with mandatory drug testing and counseling for both parents and 26 domestic violence classes for Leo to help him deal with possible anger issues. He had been charged with domestic battery a year earlier following an argument with Amanda.

Veteran Cook County criminal prosecutor Joan Perneke was assigned to the child welfare case.

With no evidence of current abuse or neglect against either Amanda or Leo, the state looked deep into their lives, searching for anything that would justify keeping the children in state custody. Psychological reports from Amanda's teen years were reviewed. Every piece of paper from the 2003 murder case was ordered from the DeWitt County courthouse.

The matter took an ironic turn one day when a call from Cook County prosecutors to the state's attorney's office in Clinton was answered by Ann Danison. She didn't let on that she knew anything about the Amanda Hamm case, but the aggressive move by the state to amass her daughter's expansive case file worried her.

Every possible avenue that could bring the children home was explored. Amanda offered to move out. Her mother offered to take the children to her home in Clinton. Nothing was acceptable to the state.

Their lawyers prepared Leo and Amanda for a long battle.

In the meantime, the parents visited the children under strict supervision of social workers and tried to reassure their daughters that everything was okay. The oldest child prayed to go home. Her younger sister acted out angrily, forgetting her potty-training progress. The new baby boy was being tended to by his aunt.

Months passed between court hearings. The holidays were a sad time with the family split between two places. The judge had denied a request that the children spend part of the holidays at the family's apartment.

For the first time, Amanda feared her daughters were losing hope; they no longer believed their parents' story that their extended stay with their aunt was due to major remodeling of their apartment.

The start of 2015 brought more demands from the state for court records from the murder case. A suggestion that Amanda had been diagnosed with schizophrenia at some point in her life resulted in more records swaps between lawyers. A counselor for Amanda received a copy of Dr. Terry Killian's report from Steve Skelton who had been monitoring the custody case, disbelieving that his former client was at the mercy of the state once again. Skelton wondered if Amanda would ever be done serving her debt to society.

Killian's report showed no signs of schizophrenia.

Amanda now worried the state would permanently sever her parental rights, using the deaths of her first three children as reason to place her two daughters and son in new homes. The judge would have final say. In April of 2015, a trial date was set for late August.

The state was poised to conduct an abbreviated version of the murder trial, with potential appearances from Maurice LaGrone and police officers who handled the investigation a dozen years earlier. Only such a gut-wrenching replay of the children's deaths would give the judge the full thrust of the state's theory: Amanda Hamm escaped the harsh punishment she deserved for her part in what many people would always view as a triple murder.

The summer was long but cooler than normal for Chicago. Amanda and Leo made daily, hour-long bus trips to visit their children. She picked up a second job as a dishwasher to help makes ends meet while she waited for summer to be over.

Chapter Forty-one

Amanda and Leo had just enough time to duck outside for a cigarette before the opening of the custody trial in Courtroom A of the Cook County Juvenile Court building. The date was Aug. 31, 2015 —18 months after the children were removed. The 16 hours she had worked each of the two previous days, combined with the drama of the courtroom, left Amanda more exhausted than usual.

Both parents were anxious to talk with their separate public defenders to find out who would be the state's first witnesses.

The small courtroom was crowded with tables for each set of lawyers—five of them representing interests of the state, the children and the parents. Some of the materials they had gathered dated back several decades. A single bench at the back of each side of the courtroom accommodated auxiliary staff for the lawyers and the occasional reporter who took an interest in a juvenile proceeding.

Associate Judge Kottaras summoned lawyers into the courtroom for a conversation on the status of the case. What was the common ground the two sides had found and what divisions remained? He wanted to know.

Assistant State's Attorney Pernecke spoke first, informing the judge that some negotiations had taken place, but the two sides couldn't agree on a stipulation of the facts about what had occurred on Sept. 2, 2003. The defense version lacked critical details the judge would need, she said, to form "a full picture, a full history of both these people and the children."

The "full picture" the state was seeking was actually only a partial portrait that left out elements that could provide the judge with the critical insight needed to make a fair decision, argued Leo's attorney, Lisa Dedmond. Besides, some of the records the state sought to admit dated back to 1968 and were nothing more than a maneuver by prosecutors "to dirty up" the parents, she said.

Carol Casey, with the Office of the Cook County Public Guardian representing the children, sided with the state.

"The court has to understand the facts from 12 years ago that are not going away. They're really bad," Casey told the judge.

The state had people lined up ready to testify, Pernecke confirmed.

The judge was willing to make one effort to resolve the matter short of a trial.

"It seems like we were working towards a resolution and here we are at a trial," said Kottaras, offering to sit down in a conference room with lawyers if it would advance negotiations.

Lawyers opted to talk without the judge. Their conversation was brief. It produced no significant agreement.

Sitting in the lobby area across from the toys and TV used to keep children occupied as they awaited court appearances, Amanda felt her sense of dread deepen as she thought about the testimony and evidence she may be forced to revisit in the courtroom. Pictures of her car sinking into the lake, the last portrait of her dead children—it was all too much to think about, but something she may have to endure as she fought losing three more children born to her since her acquittal on murder charges.

She questioned whether she should have become a mother again.

Yet in a final conversation with their lawyers, Amanda and Leo were firm in their refusal to accept a partial stipulation of the facts. It was time for a trial.

Amanda and Leo sat at opposite ends of the defense table. They each had their own lawyer to avoid any possible conflict that may arise from their separate custody rights as parents.

In her opening remarks, Pernecke laid out the basis for the state's petition to take the children.

The case did not start in February 2014 when a doctor recognized Amanda and called the state child abuse hotline, said the prosecutor. Or in 2013 when Amanda sought an order of protection against Leo for hitting her. The case was not rooted in her August 2013 accusations to police that Leo stole $100 from her to buy drugs and threatened to harm her.

Central to the case was Amanda's pattern of choosing the wrong man whose propensity for verbal and physical abuse, combined with a lack of motivation to work and support a family, always ended badly for her and her children, said the prosecutor.

Pernecke argued that the September 2002 chance meeting of Maurice and Amanda in central Illinois also was not the genesis of the custody case a dozen years later in a Cook County courtroom. Choosing the worst claims against Maurice—some of them unsubstantiated in his murder case—Pernecke pieced together an image of a cocaine-loving gangbanger who delighted in deliberately tormenting Ware's first three children.

In an entirely new twist to any theory previously put forth by the state in the murder cases, Pernecke suggested something Amanda had said to a mental health worker after a suicide attempt at age 19 was at the root of the custody battle. It was in 1995, the prosecutor said, that Amanda conceived of the plot to drown her not-yet-born children, linking the suicide attempt to the deaths of the three children eight years later.

The plot to kill her children was hatched when she said she planned to drive into a lake, the prosecutor theorized. And there was no doubt Amanda had the lake in her hometown in mind for the plot, he continued, because "when you're from Clinton, Illinois, that's the lake you're talking about."

In their next phone call after the hearing, neither Amanda nor her mother could recall the statement supposedly made during Amanda's second suicide attempt as a teenager.

Amanda's history of choosing the wrong partners, with a possible result of harm to her three living children, represented "a freight train of evidence" that could not be ignored, said Pernecke. The state's position of anticipatory neglect—the belief that the children were at risk, based on their mother's past failures—was a reasonable and appropriate legal stance, she argued.

In closing her remarks, the prosecutor took several long strides across the courtroom in what she represented as the 26.5 feet Amanda would have had to walk, wade or swim from the shore to get back to the car containing her drowning children.

In her short opening statement, Casey of the guardian's office said the custody proceeding was "not about murder or redemption" but about her clients—the children.

Amanda's and Leo's pasts were relevant to the present because Leo's criminal history and Amanda's conviction for child endangerment brought forward issues that demand examination, she said.

In her opening remarks, Leo's attorney, Dedmond, acknowledged Amanda and Leo had experienced problems in their relationship. But the custody dispute began with the doctor's call to the state welfare agency.

With no signs of abuse or neglect noted after a home visit, the two Ware daughters were taken, a task described as "damned near impossible" by a worker who saw the screaming and distraught children, said Dedmond.

The defense lawyer also pointed out that police who had been called to the Ware apartment because of domestic incidents never found it necessary to call DCFS. The Ware children, she said, want to go home.

Chapter Forty-two

The drama of death and despair that had marked the lives of Amanda and the six children she bore had come full circle in the dozen years since her car rolled into the lake. No more visible sign of that reality could be found than when former state police sergeant Ben Halloran walked into the Chicago courtroom.

The interview of Amanda by police while she was a psychiatric patient was the focus of testimony from the officer who had been retired two years now. Halloran admitted he had sometimes become aggravated during the multiple interviews of Amanda.

"It was more out of frustration," he said. "The evidence was so clear from the investigation that this was a murder and she was withholding information from us."

Dedmond's co-counsel, Steven Dore, objected to the former detective's opinion.

"This is not a murder trial," said the judge, allowing the answer to stand.

"It sure seems like it," Dore muttered under his breath.

Halloran's voice cracked as he recounted Amanda's description of the car and her children sinking from sight.

"She said they made no efforts to rescue the kids. They stood in front of the car for one to two minutes and watched the children drown," said Halloran.

When the trial continued Sept. 3, it was the 12th anniversary of Kyleigh's death. Amanda came to the court facility early in the day for a mandated drug test but then went home to be alone. She wouldn't hear the testimony of William Smith, the Chicago police officer who responded to her call for help at the Ware apartment in April 2012.

Smith testified Amanda told him her husband had struck her with an open hand during a yelling match that turned physical.

"She was upset, crying at times," said Smith, several days shy of his 20-year mark with the department. He recalled redness and swelling below Amanda's right ear.

Smith said he spotted Leo Ware a short distance from the apartment and confronted him about the domestic dispute. Leo was "business like," Smith said, and didn't deny the argument.

And did the officer ask the suspect if he had any gang affiliations, Assistant State's Attorney Gina Perdue inquired?

Before Smith could answer, Dedmond was on her feet, objecting to questions about Leo and gangs. "This is simply to dirty him up," she said.

Perdue insisted Leo's criminal history was part of the state's petition against the parents, making any of Leo's legal missteps fair game. "Gang affiliation is an indicator of many dangerous things," she suggested.

The judge sided with the state and allowed Officer Smith to answer.

"He admitted he was a Conservative Vice Lord," he said, noting Leo was 46 years old at the time of his affiliation with the street gang.

The domestic dispute that led to charges against Leo was not reported to state child welfare people, the officer confirmed. "The children didn't appear to be in distress." The charges against Leo were dropped later when Amanda didn't follow through with an order of protection she had sought following the argument.

The scene at Clinton Lake came alive for Judge Kottaras as Rick Hawn, also now retired from his job as a DeWitt County detective, summarized the most incriminating elements of his investigation. There was no reason for the car to accidentally end up in the lake, he concluded.

Hawn's prior observations about Amanda's reactions to her sons' bodies as they lay lifeless in the emergency room were repeated for the family court judge.

"Her voice was monotone, not smooth or natural. She was searching for words. I've been in many situations with mothers who are grieving the loss of a child. They wail and their words are mournful," said Hawn.

Amanda's words whispered to her boyfriend as they embraced in the hospital hallway— "don't worry, stay strong"—were repeated for Judge Kottaras.

Before Hawn took the witness stand a second day, Dore informed the judge Amanda was still ill and would not join her husband in court.

In his questions, Dore tried to draw out every fact that could place Amanda in a positive light, or at least lighten the dark shadows the state had cast on her. Her tender remarks to her sons as she saw them for the last time in the emergency room and her fear of being under water—two facts captured in multiple police reports—were acknowledged by the retired officer.

The scene at the central Illinois lake—more than a two-hour drive from the Chicago courtroom—was set for the judge by large aerial photos taken by Hawn during his investigation.

The replay of the murder trials continued with Timothy Collins, the 5-foot 3-inch former deputy who was one of the first officers to rush into the lake.

The children "were all lifeless, limp" when they were pulled from the car, he said. Their mother stood on the sidelines, Collins remembered. "I didn't see her do anything around the vehicle."

Among the more poignant images presented in the custody trial was a Collins recollection from the reenactment police conducted at the lake three days after the drownings. As the car was lowered into the water, he spotted "15 to 20 tiny handprints" in the car's back window.

Three weeks later, the lawyers and the Wares were back in court for closing arguments in the custody trial.

The state held firm to its contention Amanda and Leo had abused and neglected their three children. Old mistakes had been replaced by new ones that could put their children in the same type of danger that ended the lives of siblings they never met, said Pernecke.

"She has not changed the pattern. This freight train of evidence is bearing down on three children who must be protected," she said.

Dedmond tried to shift the focus away from 2003 and towards more recent segments of the Wares' lives as parents.

Before the state intervened in their lives, the family was doing well, she said, with both parents working and Leo leading drug rehab support meetings. "What we have here is speculation," Dedmond told the judge, reminding him the state was obligated to provide proof the children were abused and neglected.

Judge Kottaras said he'd announce his decision in a week.

On Nov. 6, 2015, an anxious group that included two reporters and lawyers who supported the defense and the state waited outside the courtroom. The notoriety of the Ware case was recognized by the judge and lawyers unaccustomed to media scrutiny of their work.

Kottaras delayed a lunch recess, opting instead to call the Ware case and satisfy everyone's curiosity about his ruling.

Leo Ware took his seat next to his lawyer and Amanda sank into a spot on the bench behind the defense table. Both parents looked exhausted, ready for the ordeal to be over.

Before he read his four–page decision to a courtroom silent and heavy with anticipation, the judge handed copies of his text to the clerk to distribute to reporters.

Quoting from a report on Amanda's 2003 hospitalization after the drownings, Kottaras said "she has a tendency to be addicted to drugs, alcohol and abusive relationships. She is often physically and emotionally abusive to others and likes to provoke others to get a reaction."

Kottaras incorrectly described the hospital stay as "one of her psychiatric hospitalizations after being released from prison for endangering the life of her three children when she and her then boyfriend drove their car into a lake, drowning all three of them." Amanda had not been in a psychiatric hospital since her release from prison.

The judge went on to emphasize police interviews showing Amanda admitted in the hospital that she lied to police but was now saying it was not Maurice's fault the children died. Much of Kottaras' ruling was based on testimony he understood as he heard it from the former DeWitt County and state police officers or read in snippets from their reports.

"I am not here to re-litigate the past case involving the death of her first three children but to consider the judgment and behavior as factors as they relate to the three Ware children," he said.

Amanda's extensive mental health history and her admissions to using drugs, combined with her poor choice of partners, were two strikes against her, in Kottaras' mind. Her unwavering declaration that her first three children's deaths were accidental was strike number three.

"Let me also state, make no mistake, by no stretch of the imagination was the drowning death of mother's oldest three children an accident," the judge opined. After all, the jumbo photo of the Clinton Lake boat ramp displayed at one of his hearings clearly showed "there was no reason for the car to be at the boat ramp—none at all."

Leo Ware did not fare much better in the ruling. His record of drugs and domestic violence against Amanda did not impress the judge. Add to that Leo's ready acceptance of Amanda's version of the deaths of her first three children and he had a third strike as well.

Even without the drowning case, the state had stockpiled enough evidence to convince the judge the three children were in a dangerous environment if they lived with their parents.

"It has been argued that the three Ware children look fine. We do not have to wait for the injuries," the judge said, concluding the state had proven its case.

Amanda and Leo showed no reaction when they heard the ruling that went against them. They were not surprised. They left the courthouse through separate doors.

They returned to their routines of visiting the kids, working jobs that never paid enough to cover what the family needed in its divided state, working to please social workers and mental health professionals who continually monitored their progress for the court.

In June of 2016, Judge Kottaras said he saw some progress, yet Amanda and Leo remained "unfit and unwilling" to care for their children. He also said Amanda was "unable" to be a good mother. And so was Leo so long as he tested positive for drugs.

There was another condition the judge needed to be met. Amanda would have to admit to playing a part in the death of her three children. She continued to minimize that role during her therapy sessions and "deceived and outright conned" her counselor, the judge said, by failing to admit her "responsibility for the drowning murders of her first three children."

"That sounds like Mrs. Ware has put blinders on to that event in order to survive her everyday life and go on," the judge scolded.

Amanda covered her face with her hands and cried.

Epilogue

The judge's ruling, while a severe blow to Amanda and Leo's fight for custody, stopped short of an even more severe outcome that would permanently sever all parental rights. And the parents retained access to free state services while the parties worked toward a lasting resolution.

The Ware children were settling into their third year living with their aunt as attorneys for both sides began talks that could end the state's involvement in the case. The judge had made it abundantly clear he did not favor sending the children back to Amanda and Leo—whether together or as single parents.

A guardianship where the aunt would become the decision-maker for the three children while Amanda and Leo kept visitation rights was proposed. For the parents, such an arrangement offered a positive change: an end to DCFS involvement in their lives.

On February 20, 2018, Amanda and Leo gathered with lawyers for the state and defense before Judge Kottaras. The group crowded at the bench in front of the judge, a sign the hearing would be brief.

For the first time in almost four years, everyone signaled their agreement as to what should occur in the best interests of the children, now ages 7, 6 and 3. The aunt told the judge she was willing to continue caring for her two nieces and nephew who would live in the house she shared with her school age son.

With no sign of emotion, Amanda and Leo concurred.

"Mother is in agreement," Amanda's lawyer told the judge. "Father agrees," echoed Leo's lawyer.

The children's relatives could work together as a family to raise the children.

"We can say it takes a village," the judge said. "We can say a family has to come together and you have done so. I think your track record speaks for itself."

The 20-minute hearing ended abruptly. The guardianship had been finalized.

An atmosphere of relief and satisfaction hung over the crowd of lawyers and social workers who mingled afterwards outside the courtroom. The resolution, while far from perfect in the minds of Amanda and Leo, was satisfactory to those who negotiated difficult family separations every day.

Amanda quickly left the courthouse, eager to get back to a part of her life that was more rewarding than the judicial system, hoping one day her children would tell a judge they'd like to live with their mom. That she one day could prove herself worthy of motherhood. And of forgiveness.

For now, she had accomplished a long-time goal of getting a full-time job with benefits, working for a food service company. She also kept her second job with a caterer.

Leo vowed to keep fighting to regain custody of the children.

At a memorial service organized by little Christopher's father on the 15th anniversary of the drownings, flowers were laid at each of the three graves.

The three fathers, now middle-aged men, acknowledged the bouts of grief that still struck them hard on certain days. Forgiveness was also on the minds of some family members.

Quoting author Jonathan Lockwood Huie to a reporter, Amanda's mother Ann Powers held out hope that her daughter would be forgiven for her failure to save the children. "Forgive not because they deserve forgiveness, but because you deserve peace," she said.

For his part, Maurice LaGrone Jr. — now 42 years old — was adjusting to his transfer from a maximum-security prison to a medium-security facility in western Illinois. Family members had kept him apprised of Amanda's custody battle.

Sitting behind a Plexiglas security window, he expressed regret that his actions 14 years earlier were still creating turmoil for her. Meanwhile he held hope a lawyer somewhere would somehow find reasons to reopen his case. A sentence closer to the 10 years Amanda received would be equal justice, Maurice suggested.

But in the next breath, he said he understood the jury's murder verdict in his case.

"The fact that three kids was involved," Maurice acknowledged, "was just too much for everybody."

Acknowledgements

We express our gratitude to those who helped us compile the large volume of materials and information to ensure the most accurate account of this sad story that has changed so many lives. Without the cooperation of those closest to the case, the level of detail of what took place over a dozen years would be far less complete.

Many of the photos that help illustrate this work first appeared in *The Pantagraph* in Bloomington, Illinois. Photo editor David Proeber was a terrific source of support as were other colleagues at this first-class community newspaper.

Our thanks to Rose Marie Harris and the Washington writers' group for their encouragement, advice and critical review of our early efforts. The input of this accomplished group was invaluable.

We appreciate greatly the patience and support of our families during this long endeavor. Their assistance with uncooperative computers and other challenges related to technology that forever exceeds our common abilities kept the process from coming to a screeching halt many days.